BERIT OLAM
Studies in Hebrew Narrative & Poetry

Ezra
and
Nehemiah

Gordon F. Davies

David W. Cotter, O.S.B.
Editor

Jerome T. Walsh
Chris Franke
Associate Editors

A Michael Glazier Book
THE LITURGICAL PRESS
Collegeville, Minnesota

A Michael Glazier Book published by The Liturgical Press

Cover design by Ann Blattner

1   2   3   4   5   6   7   8

Library of Congress Cataloging-in-Publication Data

Davies, Gordon F. (Gordon Fay)
    Ezra and Nehemiah / Gordon F. Davies ; David W. Cotter, editor ;
Jerome T. Walsh, Chris Franke, associate editors.
        p.   cm. — (Berit olam)
    "A Michael Glazier book."
    Includes bibliographical references and index.
    ISBN 0-8146-5049-X (alk. paper)
    1. Bible. O.T. Ezra—Criticism, interpretation, etc. 2. Bible.
O.T. Nehemiah—Criticism, interpretation, etc. I. Cotter, David W.
II. Walsh, Jerome T., 1942–   . III. Franke, Chris. IV. Title.
V. Series.
BS1355.2.D38   1998
222' .7077—dc21   98-24496
                                                                    CIP

To Robert, my father (1924–1974) and Adair, my sister (1952–1993)
—speaking together the language of the celestial discourse.

CONTENTS

FOREWORD

My thanks go to St Augustine's Seminary of Toronto and the Archdiocese of Toronto who so willingly granted me a sabbatical to complete this book, and to the Catholic Biblical Association whose Young Scholars Fellowship helped finance it. The École Biblique de Jérusalem and Campion Hall, Oxford gave me shelter and much stimulating company. Sara Japhet, Étienne Nodet, Paolo Garuti, and Hugh Williamson kindly offered their views on my work. I will always be intellectually indebted to Charles Conroy whose thesis direction helped me with my first book and whose friendship supported me with the second.

Working with the proofs, I benefited from the keen assistance of staff and students at St. Augustine's Seminary: Paul Dobson, Edwin Gonsalves, Geoffrey Kerslake, Steve Lape, Tim McCauley, Mark Robson, and especially for the painstaking work on the indexes Kirsten Caspersen, Johanna Moloughney, and Jean Walsh. I am very grateful to them for helping me draw the work on the book to a close.

26 September 1997
Feast of the Canadian Martyrs

ABBREVIATIONS

AB	Anchor Bible
ABD	*The Anchor Bible Dictionary*
AnBib	Analecta Biblica
BTB	*Biblical Theology Bulletin*
CBQ	*Catholic Biblical Quarterly*
IB	*The Interpreter's Bible*
JBL	*Journal of Biblical Literature*
JR	*Journal of Religion*
JSOT.S	Journal for the Study of the Old Testament, Supplement Series
KAT	Kommentar zum Alten Testament
MT	Masoretic (Hebrew) Text
NCBC	New Century Bible Commentary
NEB.AT	Die Neue Echter Bibel. Kommentar zum Alten Testament mit der Einheitsübersetzung
NIC	The New International Commentary
OTGu	Old Testament Guides
OTL	Old Testament Library
OTMes	Old Testament Message
QSJ	Que sais-je?
SBL.DS	Society of Biblical Literature Dissertation Series
SBL.SS	Society of Biblical Literature Semeia Studies
ScrHie	Scripta Hierosolymitana. Jerusalem
StTh	*Studia Theologica*
ThQ	*Theologische Quartalschrift*
VT.S	Supplements to *Vetus Testamentum*
WBC	Word Biblical Commentary
WMANT	Wissenschaftliche Monographien zum Alten und Neuen Testament
ZAW	*Zeitschrift für die alttestamentliche Wissenschaft*

INTRODUCTION

Rhetorical Criticism and History

It is odd that we know more about earlier moments of biblical history than we do of the long and eventful span from about 538 B.C.E. to 63 B.C.E., that is, the return from Exile to the beginning of Roman rule in Palestine. Ezra–Nehemiah is the main biblical source of information about the two hundred years in which Persia dominated this age, from Cyrus II's conquest of Babylon in 539 to Alexander's victory in 333, and the events in Ezra–Nehemiah cover no more than half that time. Large portions of the Bible were redacted into their final version then, and studying Ezra–Nehemiah can help us understand the principles of that faith-forming enterprise. The period also witnessed the emergence of Judaism properly so called, distinct in certain important ways from the pre-Exilic Israelite religion. Ezra and Nehemiah can accurately be called two of the most important figures in Jewish history.[1]

An inquisitive investigator of our text will quickly ask why it was written. With Chronicles, it comprises a third history of Israel, besides the deuteronomistic history (Joshua–Kings) and the final redaction of the Pentateuch. The reply must depend on the much-discussed relation of Ezra–Nehemiah to Chronicles, and whether the law that Ezra proclaimed was some part or form of the Pentateuch.

We will dare to suggest reasons for Ezra–Nehemiah's approach at the end of this book. We begin by noticing its self-presentation as a history of some kind, with various marks of that genre: dates, the names of historical figures, lists, genealogies and quotations. In the book, documentary evidence gives impulse to events more than any theophany does; indeed, YHWH never intervenes directly in the action.

However, the book poses severe problems for the reader who would use it as a source for the history of the Reconstruction. The sec-

---

[1] Robert North, "Ezra," *The Anchor Bible Dictionary*, eds. David Noel Freedman et al. (New York: Doubleday, 1992) 2:726, citing George Widengren.

ond half of the Books is particularly vexed (Ezra 7–10; Nehemiah 7–13).

The following are just a few of the historiographical and textual issues. We do not understand the relation of the "people of the land" to the Samaritans. If Ezra was a Persian minister of Jewish affairs why did he have no successor? The duplication between the end of Chronicles (2 Chron 36:22-23) and the beginning of Ezra (1:1-3a) complicates rather than solves the debate about a common authorship. How much of Ezra's Memoir and Nehemiah's is true autobiography? It is not clear who came first, Ezra or Nehemiah, or when Ezra journeyed to Jerusalem, or how many times. Which Artaxerxes commissioned him?

Scholars are quite confident that Nehemiah's return from Exile occurred in 445. The traditional view places Ezra before Nehemiah, with the former arriving from Babylon in "the seventh year of King Artaxerxes" (Ezra 7:7-8). If Artaxerxes was the first of that name (465–424) the date would be 458 B.C.E. But discrepancies make some scholars suspect it was Artaxerxes II (404–360), so that Ezra's return would have been in 398, after Nehemiah's. Others say that the difficulties are best explained by dating Ezra's journey to 428, positing an unsupported correction in the text of Ezra 7:7-8 from "the seventh year" to "the thirty-seventh" year. The 398 date held a slight consensus earlier, but recent studies tend to return to the traditional dating and order of events.[2]

In a further complication, the material on each leader is interwoven although the men themselves almost never appear together. Early scholars like C. C. Torrey and Wilhelm Rudolph tried to resolve the problems of the dating and the mixing of the Ezra material with that of Nehemiah (Ezra 7–10; Nehemiah 8–10, and Nehemiah 1–7; 11–13) by reconstructing an original three-step work, one part for each of the post-exilic leaders. Zerubbabel would have been given the mission to raise the Temple, Ezra reinstituted the Law, and Nehemiah rebuilt the walls of Jerusalem. All three completed their tasks despite opposition and each time a great assembly celebrated the end of the labor. The reconstructed text would read like this:

> A. Zerubbabel (538–515 B.C.E.)
>   1. Reconstruction of the Temple (Ezra 1:1–6:15)
>   2. Assembly for celebration and Passover (Ezra 6:16-22)

---

[2] For much of this text-critical summary see Mark A. Throntveit, *When Kings Speak: Royal Speech and Royal Prayer in Chronicles*, SBL.DS 93, ed. J. J. M. Roberts (Atlanta, Ga.: Scholars, 1987) 1–2, here citing Derek Kidner; and H. G. M. Williamson, *Ezra, Nehemiah*, WBC 16, eds. David A. Hubbard et al. (Waco, Texas: Word Books, 1985) xxxix–xliv.

B. Ezra (458–457 B.C.E.)
  1. Reinstitution of the Law (Ezra 7–8; Neh 7:73b–8:18; Ezra 9–10)
  2. Assembly for fasting and confession (Neh 9–10)
C. Nehemiah (446–433 B.C.E.)
  1. Reconstruction of the walls and repopulating of Jerusalem (Neh 1:1–7:73a; 11:1–12:26)
  2. Assembly and Dedication (Neh 12:27–13:3)
Appendix: Cultic Reforms of Nehemiah (Neh 13:4-31)

Aside from continuing debates about the priority of Ezra or Nehemiah, various refinements of this position have dominated text-critical approaches ever since. All of them presuppose intensive redaction. Rhetorical criticism does not judge such a reconstructed sequence, but it may shed light on the principles for the ordering such as we find it now in a text that calls itself a history but does not seem to follow chronological criteria.

Historical narrative or historiography is itself a genre and one should not invent a false choice in Ezra–Nehemiah between 'literature' and 'history'.[3] Rhetorical criticism can be applied to any form of communication, including history. The historian's attribution of meaning and relations to events is itself a rhetorical act in the sense that we will define and use that term. Many scholars point to the numerous documents in the book and conclude that part of its purpose is archival. That is probably true, but no one suggests that record-preservation is the only impulse behind it.[4] It is not a running summary of events and statements. Nor is it like other historical narratives in the Bible. A rhetorical-critical analysis can help point to these differences.

Clearly the book is not written along modern lines of cohesive sequence. Big shifts in time and place are sometimes made smooth, sometimes left rough. The central issues and the organizing principles are theological. The editor paid close attention to the relations between the two men Ezra and Nehemiah, between the major units aligned in

---

[3] See Sara Japhet, "'History' and 'Literature' in the Persian Period: The Restoration of the Temple," in *Ah, Assyria . . . Studies in Assyrian History and Ancient Near Eastern Historiography Presented to Hayim Tadmor*, eds. Mordechai Cogan and Israel Eph'al. ScrHie 33 (Jerusalem: Magnes Press, 1991) 174–88.

[4] Tamara Cohn Eskenazi, "The Structure of Ezra–Nehemiah and the Integrity of the Book," *JBL* 107 (1988) 644, points to Chronicles with its bold rewriting of sacred traditions and also 1 Esdras as indications that the pious preservation of ancient texts and traditions was not the only motivation of the scribes, or an impediment to their redactional activity.

parallel structure, and between past and current events. A continuity of events exists on the level of divine causality.[5]

Historiography cannot be dismissed from a book that styles itself a "history."[6] Given that the author's intentions were in part historical, can we however expect the standards of modern Western historiography? We cannot suppose that it was written and preserved as history in anything like our sense, or that it was more accurate in its lost original form, which in any case never had canonical status among either Jews or Christians.[7]

Given the evident harmonizations, omissions, and duplications in the book, the burden of proof rests with those who would see its first purpose as a repository, preserving documents, lists, and genealogies for their intrinsic historical value. No doubt part of the book's motivation was archival. But if it were primarily so, we would be compelled all the more to ask why the sources were altered and arranged out of chronological sequence. We will see in what ways the book blurs the passage of time so that Ezra and Nehemiah are made contemporaries.

Scrutinizing the text as an ill-sorted scrapbook of the events of the Restoration is valuable historical work but it is not in itself exegesis. There is indeed a tension between the confessional account that we read here and the critically reconstructable history behind it, just as there is between the world-view of the Jews of that day and ours. But these cannot be isolated and studied without first laying out the indigenous theology of the book.

This commentary maintains that Ezra–Nehemiah makes theological sense in its own terms. Ezra and Nehemiah form a single work in which a range of ideas is argued. The development of these concerns shapes the disposition and, to a degree, the content of the text. A rhetorical-critical analysis can help lay this argumentation open. We can

---

[5] H. G. M. Williamson, "Post-Exilic Historiography," in *The Future of Biblical Studies: The Hebrew Bible*, eds. Richard Elliott Friedman and H. G. M. Williamson. SBL.SS 16 (Atlanta, Ga.: Scholars, 1987) 202.

[6] For example, according to D. J. A. Clines, "The Nehemiah Memoir: The Perils of Autobiography," in *What Does Eve Do To Help? And Other Readerly Questions to the Old Testament*, eds. David J. A. Clines and Philip R. Davies. JSOT.S 94 (Sheffield: JSOT Press, 1990) 124, the segment to which that name is given is the most important historiographical document in the Hebrew Bible—written within a decade of the events and in the very words of Nehemiah (Neh 1:1–7:7 [perhaps minus chapter 3]; 12:31-43; 13:4-31). It begins "The words of Nehemiah, the son of Hacaliah."

[7] Judson R. Shaver, "Ezra and Nehemiah: On the Theological Significance of Making them Contemporaries," in *Priests, Prophets and Scribes: Essays on the Formation and Heritage of Second Temple Judaism in Honour of Joseph Blenkinsopp*, eds. Eugene Ulrich et al. JSOT.S 149 (Sheffield: JSOT Press, 1992) 79.

then see better how their concept of the world and history differs from the modern.

Writing up the themes in a point-by-point list cannot account for their development in the course of the chapters. Nor is it best to divide the book into parts identified with certain leaders because, as we will see, these men are not the book's center of attention.[8] A methodology is needed that reveals the full range and progress of the book's ideas without hiding its rough seams and untidy edges. We propose rhetorical criticism as one such approach, and this book as a prolegomenon to Ezra–Nehemiah studies. Part of its novelty is that few rhetorical analyses exist of entire biblical books, especially those that are not poetry.[9]

Rhetorical criticism is not the only approach for reading Ezra–Nehemiah. But the leaders bring the people around to their plans, and they do so without the violence of coercion or the grace of any theophany. Their strategies of argument to achieve their goals are a pass-key to the theological understructure of the book. To apply rhetorical criticism at its most straightforward we will concentrate on the public discourses and prayers. The very quantity of orations, letters, and prayers in Ezra–Nehemiah reflects its emphasis on the word. This approach to Ezra–Nehemiah fits it as a text of declamation more than action.

---

[8] Sara Japhet, "Sheshbazzar and Zerubbabel—Against the Background of the Historical and Religious Tendencies of Ezra–Nehemiah," *ZAW* 94 (1982) 94 points out that Ezra–Nehemiah has a specific concept of history, revealed in the structure of the book. The whole period divides into two. In each part there are two leading personalities acting side by side. In the first period (in Ezra 1–6) these are Zerubbabel and Jeshua, in the second (in Ezra 7–Nehemiah 13), Nehemiah and Ezra. This is true but incomplete since the argumentation will progressively remove attention—and theological weight—from the leaders.

[9] See Pietro Bovati and Roland Meynet, *Le livre d'Amos*, Collection Rhétorique Biblique 2 (Paris: Cerf, 1994); Georg Braulik, *Die Mittel deuteronomischer Rhetorik*, AnBib 68 (Rome: Pontifical Biblical Institute, 1978); Rodney K. Duke, *The Persuasive Appeal of the Chronicler: A Rhetorical Analysis*, JSOT.S 88, eds. David J. A. Clines and Philip R. Davies (Sheffield: Almond Press, 1990); Robert H. O'Connell, *The Rhetoric of the Book of Judges*, VT.S 62, eds. J. A. Emerton et al. (Leiden, New York, and Cologne: E. J. Brill, 1996); Mark A. Throntveit, *When Kings Speak: Royal Speech and Royal Prayer in Chronicles*, SBL.DS 93, ed. J. J. M. Roberts (Atlanta, Ga.: Scholars, 1987) on Chronicles; Phyllis Trible, *Rhetorical Criticism: Context, Method and the Book of Jonah*, Guides to Biblical Scholarship, ed. Gene M. Tucker (Minneapolis: Fortress, 1994); Ben Witherington III, *Conflict & Community in Corinth: A Socio-Rhetorical Commentary on 1 and 2 Corinthians* (Grand Rapids: Eerdmans, 1995). They differ on the nature of biblical rhetorical criticism.

Israel's paradigm of revelation is shifting here from "the sanctity of the oral to the sanctity of the written."[10] The Davidic dynasty has fallen and cannot transmit God's will. The classical age of the prophets is over. The listless and dejected post-Exilic society will be reconstructed on the written word. With Ezra's reforms the text of Scripture becomes an open book and a canon, a publicly accessible source of grace and power to be shared equally with all who are capable of understanding (Neh 8:2). Ezra–Nehemiah depicts faithful life as the "actualization" of the sacred text by the whole community.

The purpose of rhetorical criticism is to explain not the source but the power of the text as a unitary message.[11] Rhetoric can be broadly defined as the "art of persuasion" whose "duty and office [it is] to apply reason to imagination for the better moving of the will."[12]

The nature of any historiography can be called rhetorical; the description is not limited to those with theological interests.[13] It is so because it attributes meaning and interconnection to events by virtue of whatever interpretive tools the historian has adopted. A scholar of the rhetoric of historiography defines a historical work as "a verbal structure in the form of a narrative prose discourse that purports to be a model or icon of past structures and processes in the interest of *explaining what they were by representing* them."[14] The presuppositions of a historian and the formal coherence and principles of analysis of the explanation of a "course of history" make such writing rhetorical.[15] Indeed,

> the basic rhetorical perspective is simply this: all utterance, except perhaps the mathematical formula, is aimed at influencing a particular audience at a particular time and place, even if the only audience is the speaker or writer himself; any utterance may be interpreted rhetorically by being studied in terms of its situation—within its original milieu or

[10] A central point in Tamara Cohn Eskenazi, *In an Age of Prose. A Literary Approach to Ezra–Nehemiah* (Atlanta, Ga.: Scholars, 1988), quoted here at 191.

[11] George A. Kennedy, *New Testament Interpretation through Rhetorical Criticism* (Chapel Hill and London: University of North Carolina Press, 1984) 159.

[12] Francis Bacon, quoted in Richard A. Lanham, *A Handlist of Rhetorical Terms. A Guide for Students of English Literature* (Berkeley: University of California Press, 1968) 87.

[13] See, for example, Hayden White, "Rhetoric and History," in *Theories of History*, eds. Hayden White and Frank E. Manuel. William Andrews Clark Memorial Library Seminar Papers (Los Angeles: University of California Press, 1978) 3–25.

[14] Hayden White, *Metahistory: The Historical Imagination in the Nineteenth Century* (Baltimore: Johns Hopkins University Press, 1973) 2.

[15] Duke, *The Persuasive Appeal of the Chronicler* 31.

even within its relationship to any reader or hearer—as if it were an argument.[16]

History, literary criticism, and the social sciences are apt to look at a text as though it were a map of the author's mind on a particular subject. Rhetorical criticism looks on it as the embodiment of an intention that affects the audience and is affected by it. Structure, too, is a result of this intention. This concern for audience, intention, and structure is the mark of rhetorical criticism. It recognizes the philosophical observation that the meaning of language lies in the way we use it.[17]

Rhetorical criticism differs from some other approaches in insisting that a text reveal the context. Especially in its modern form it looks as much to the process of interpretation by the reader or listener as to the mechanics of creation by the author or speaker. The "message" of a text is a compound of elements of time, place, motivation, and response that shape effects on both the communicator and the communicants.[18] Rhetoric is not a set of rules on "how to speak" or topics to help one know "what to say." Rhetorical criticism is interested in figures of speech insofar as "they are means of persuasion, and more especially, means of creating 'presence' (i.e., bringing to the mind of the hearer things that are not immediately present)" otherwise.[19] It involves our taking seriously our own responsibility as readers, aware that a biblical book like any communication is a collaborative work— the text created by the author and the realization accomplished by the reader or listener.

This attention to the audience means that rhetorical criticism has an eye to two groups, the audience within the text and us, the readers of Ezra–Nehemiah today who examine the relations between them and the speaker and yet also experience the persuasiveness of the text in our own right. The effect on us is a compound of our own reaction and our observation of that of the first listeners. A text cannot be "understood" apart from these various layers of results. Of course much of the effect on the original ancient audience is impossible for us

---

[16] Thomas Sloane, "Rhetoric: Rhetoric in literature," *Encyclopaedia Britannica*, ed. Philip W. Goetz. (15th ed. Chicago: Encyclopaedia Britannica Co. Ltd., 1991) 26:758–762, at 762.

[17] This is not the place to trace the relation of rhetorical criticism to the philosophy of language of Wittgenstein and of Austin and Searle. Chaïm Perelman, "Rhetoric in philosophy: the new rhetoric," *Encyclopaedia Britannica*, ed. Philip W. Goetz. 15th ed. 26:762–764 has interesting reflections on his own work as a response to the charge of Logical Empiricism that all judgments of value are illogical.

[18] Sloane, "Rhetoric," 758.

[19] Perelman, "Rhetoric in philosophy," 762.

to know. The author's own purpose is also now a mystery: all that can be observed is the intention communicated through the text. Prudence and "the self-conscious sense of historical perspective which is part of our modern intellectual equipment [can help] against the danger of modernization of the Bible."[20]

This attention to the continuing reception of the arguments is not unlike canonical criticism's advertence to the believing community, but it is broader: anyone can be spoken to persuasively in a describable way, regardless of their beliefs. This alertness to the various audiences opens the way to the helpful distinction between the decisions being advocated by the speaker and its theology. One need not accept the desired conclusions, such as racial segregation, to trace and appreciate the persuasive effect of the theological argument.

An advantage of rhetorical criticism is that this scrutiny of the audiences in context favors the search for the ideas and structures that are indigenous to the culture of the text. (At the end of the book we will discuss the questions for which this analysis of Ezra–Nehemiah has no answer.) This is especially interesting here because, unlike parts of the Pentateuch, the events of this book owe nothing to oral legends inherited from an earlier culture.

We are not assuming that the ancient Jews thought rhetorically as we do or as the Greeks did any more than one must believe they understood canonicity and historiography as we do in order to study the creation of the text and the events it describes. It is handy to use the Greeks' terminology only because, although they did not invent rhetoric, they did invent the teaching of it.[21]

No trick harmonization could cancel the existence in Ezra–Nehemiah of confusing scribal errors and glosses. Rhetorical criticism does not depend on coherence in the plot. Indeed, the events of the book do move erratically from the restoration and repopulation of the city to the building of the altar and the Temple to the declaration of the Law and the making of a common agreement. A rhetorical approach does not look at the plot development, characterization, or other elements of narrativity whose roughness makes Ezra–Nehemiah a frustration to read. As we will see, much of the text is not logical or well-fitted, but then persuasive communication often is not. We will concentrate on persuasive effects, for which logic, coherence, and elegance are not necessary.

---

[20] Robert Alter, "How Convention Helps Us Read: The Case of the Bible's Annunciation Type-Scene," _Prooftexts_ 3 (1983) 117.

[21] Olivier Reboul, _La rhétorique_, QSJ 2133 (5th ed. Paris: Presses Universitaires de France, 1996) 6.

As to reconstructing a more original text, rhetoric works on the principle of "non-paraphrase." A text cannot be rearranged or paraphrased and remain the same rhetorical work. Any change replaces it with another piece of rhetoric that does not have the same sense or effect. The basis of an argument is inseparable from its form with all that it entails, however vague, summary, or emotive.[22] Theoretically one could write a rhetorical analysis of the text of Ezra–Nehemiah as one believes it read originally. But that would be another commentary because it would be about another piece of persuasive discourse altogether.

The task of rhetorical criticism is to examine the three parts of the relationship between the speaker and the audience. These are the strategies, the situations, and the effects.[23] The strategies are the various kinds of arguments that will be explained as they occur in the text. The effects are potential as well as real, ideal as well as actual, long-range as well as immediate.

As for the rhetorical situation, it must be examined afresh with every speech in a text and goes beyond the *Sitz im Leben* of historical criticism. It has to do with the relationship between people and their environment, and with the origin and goal of the communication. Its three constituents are the "exigency" of the moment, the intended audience that is to be persuaded, and the constraints that influence the rhetor and can be brought to bear upon the audience. The "exigency" is the circumstance to which the audience is called upon to make some response. The situation depends not only on historical, social, or cultural factors, but also on the audience, the speaker, and the particular circumstances of the rhetorical act. The constraints in any rhetorical situation are made up of the persons, events, objects, and relations that are parts of the situation because they have the power to constrain the decision and action needed to modify the exigency. Sources of constraint include beliefs, attitudes, documents, facts, traditions, images, interests, motives, and the like. The rhetor too brings constraints such as personal character and style. Appropriateness or fitness—that is, how well the communication applies to the situation at hand—is thus central to rhetoric.[24]

The fundamental exigency dealt with in Ezra–Nehemiah is the incompatibility between the people's historic covenant with YHWH and

---

[22] Ibid. 75.

[23] Michael V. Fox, "The Rhetoric of Ezekiel's Vision of the Valley of the Bones," in *The Place Is Too Small For Us: The Israelite Prophets in Recent Scholarship*, ed. Robert P. Gordon. Sources for Biblical and Theological Study 5 (Winona Lake, Ind.: Eisenbrauns, 1995) 179.

[24] Lloyd F. Bitzer, "The Rhetorical Situation," *Philosophy & Rhetoric* 1 (1968) 8.

their current experience. The people of Israel, Yнwн's chosen ones, live subjected to a pagan king, their Temple destroyed and their capital desolate. Without the Temple they have no means to atone for sin.[25] The collapsed Davidic dynasty cannot be a channel for the transmission of Yнwн's will.

In all rhetoric the orator starts from theses already accepted by the audience and reinforces this adherence by various techniques of presentation. To pass to the desired conclusion the orator can use arguments of various types of association and dissociation. Associative arguments transfer the adherence from the premises already accepted to the proposed conclusions. For example, the act-person association enables one to move from the acknowledged fact that a certain act is courageous to the consequence that the agent is a courageous person.[26]

Language as Act

Words can also be actions that in the right circumstances achieve something by their very utterance. A common example of such "performative language" is a last will and testament: "I hereby leave my house to my dog." (It is often signaled by the word "hereby.") Linguists speak of the perlocutionary and illocutionary power of such utterances. An invitation to dinner has authenticity or illocutionary force if it is a genuine request to come to an actual meal. It has effectiveness or perlocutionary power only if it persuades the guests to show up. So, too, an order does not produce the intended result unless it is obeyed;[27] that is, many communications depend on a response for their effectiveness (but not for their validity). We will see several instances of play between these two kinds of "speech acts."

Three Species and Three Modes of Rhetoric

An argument is a proposition designed to make another proposition accepted.[28] Aristotle was the first to theorize that, to achieve this

---

[25] F. Charles Fensham, *The Books of Ezra and Nehemiah*, NIC, ed. R. K. Harrison (Grand Rapids: Eerdmans, 1982) 17.

[26] Perelman, "Rhetoric in philosophy," 763.

[27] G. B. Caird, *The Language and Imagery of the Bible* (Philadelphia: Westminster, 1980) 22, referring to the work of J. L. Austin.

[28] "Un argument est une proposition destinée à en faire admettre une autre": Reboul, *La rhétorique* 65.

end, rhetoric falls into three "species" or "kinds" of rhetoric: judicial, deliberate, and epideictic. Although these categories derive from the circumstances of classical Greek civic oratory they are applicable to all discourse.

The species is judicial when the author is seeking to persuade the audience to make a judgment about events that occurred in the past. It is deliberate when seeking to persuade them to take some action in the future, however immediate. Epideictic rhetoric wants them to hold or reaffirm some point of view in the present, as in the celebration or denunciation of some person or some quality. To take some psalms as clear examples, the historical psalms are generally judicial because they urge the Israelites to see their past in a certain light: "Remember the wonderful works he has done, his miracles and the judgments he uttered" (Ps 105:5). Psalms of contrition are deliberative when they intend to move Yhwh to redemptive action and the Israelite audience to conversion: "I confess my iniquity . . . Do not forsake me, O Lord!" (Ps 38:18, 21). Large parts of psalms of praise are epideictic because they celebrate the glories of Yhwh: "You have delivered my soul from death, my eyes from tears, and my feet from stumbling" (Ps 116:8).

These species of rhetoric can be in any or several of three modes corresponding to the three focuses of the speech-act: the speaker, the audience, and the speech:

- the personal character of the speaker ("ethos")
- putting the audience into a certain frame of mind ("pathos")
- the proof, actual or apparent, provided by the words of the speech ("logos").[29]

The rhetor must therefore reason logically, understand human character, and understand the emotions. Each method is used according to circumstances and will be explained in greater detail in the chapters to come.

Procedure

This will be the procedure of the book, laid out variably according to what fits best for each discourse:[30]

1. Where it is unclear, we will identify the rhetorical unit in which the discourse is set.

[29] Duke, *The Persuasive Appeal of the Chronicler* 44.
[30] Kennedy, *New Testament Interpretation* 33–38.

2. Next we will identify the audience of the discourse and the rhetorical situation.
3. The third step will be a study the arrangement of the material.
4. Next we will study the effect on the various audiences.
5. Finally, we will review the passage as a whole and judge its success.

The rhetorical unit is an argumentative whole, with a beginning, middle, and end, that affects the audiences' reasoning or imagination. The smallest rhetorical units are metaphors and parables, sayings, commandments, hymns, and so on. The next largest would be groupings of these, like the Sermon on the Mount. The largest unit is the text as a whole, either the given document or a collection of them, such as the synoptic gospels or the letters of Paul, or the whole canon.[31]

Structure

One of the complexities of Ezra–Nehemiah is that it is structured by both twos and threes.

Tamara C. Eskenazi sees a major structural device in the decree of Cyrus and the response to it (Ezra 1:1-6). The fulfilment of the decree permiting the Return and the rebuilding of the Temple entails three different movements—three movements in space from Diaspora to Jerusalem; three movements also in the sense of three groups and sets of characters; three different Persian kings as well—all bound together in their adherence to divine command and royal decree.[32]

The first movement builds the altar under Cyrus and the Temple under Darius (Ezra 1:7–6:22). The second builds up the community during Artaxerxes's reign (Ezra 7:1–10:44). The third, also under Artaxerxes, restores the city wall (Neh 1:1–7:25).

Each movement begins in Exile and culminates in Jerusalem. Each has the same broad structure, that is, preparations "over there" directly involving the Persian king, the introduction of the main characters and task, the arrival in Judah, and the implementation of the decree. Each movement focuses upon a specific component of Cyrus's mandate. A conflict hampers the execution of the task; obstacles must be overcome, and the section closes. A search of the imperial archives stops the action in Ezra 4:6-24 and another begins it again in 5:17. Ezra

---

[31] Wilhelm Wuellner, "Where is Rhetorical Criticism Taking Us?" *CBQ* 49 (1986) 455.

[32] Eskenazi, *Age of Prose* 45.

6:14 sums up all these events: "They finished their building by command of the God of Israel and by the decree of Cyrus and Darius and Artaxerxes, king of Persia," where God's "command" and the kings' "decree" are related words in the original Aramaic.[33]

Onto this pattern by threes are overlaid a number of doublings. Most obviously Ezra and Nehemiah are twinned religious and civil authorities, as Zerubbabel and Jeshua were before. Both sets of men have Persian mandates, face local resistance, and insist on separation from the people of the land. The book is so constructed that neither Ezra nor Nehemiah can be removed without the history collapsing.[34] Haggai and Zechariah are also active but invisible prophets in the beginning of Ezra. Two groups of men are on the dais for the proclamation of the Law, one to Ezra's right and one to his left (Neh 8:4). Two lists of repatriates in Ezra 2 and Nehemiah 7 embrace the three movements described above, forming what is technically called an envelope figure. Ezra 1 is thus a prologue. The Festival of Booths or Sukkoth is celebrated twice, in Ezra 3 and Nehemiah 8.

Other name lists punctuate the book, clamping the structure in place and at the same time stressing the importance of the collective effort.[35]

These and further details of the structure will become clearer as we study how people express themselves publicly in Ezra–Nehemiah in ways that give insight into the quickly changing relationship between faith, history, and leadership.

Technical Notes

The New Revised Standard Version (NRSV) is used except where a literal translation is given. The literal translations are divided into sense lines according to the criteria of Harald Schweizer.[36] A line is a

---

[33] The consonants of the word are the same: *ṭᵉm*, but the vocalization is different "perhaps to indicate the distinction between a divine and a human command": Williamson, *Ezra, Nehemiah* 72.

[34] Étienne Nodet, *Essai sur les origines du Judaïsme: de Josué aux Pharisiens* (Paris: Cerf, 1992) 254.

[35] Eskenazi, "Structure," 654. The other lists are of Ezra's companions (Ezra 8:1-14), of the men who separated from foreign wives (Ezra 10:18-44), of the builders of the wall (Neh 3:1-32), of the signatories to the pledge (Neh 10:2-29), of the settlers and settlements (Neh 11:3-36), of cultic personnel (Neh 12:1-26), of parading members of the community (Neh 12:32-42). Ezra 1:9-11 is a list of the vessels brought back from Exile.

[36] "Wovon reden die Exegeten? Zum Verständnis der Exegese als verstehender und deskriptiver Wissenschaft," *ThQ* 164 (1984) 161–185, at 174–175.

unit of meaning with a discrete function. It has only one finite verb or it can be nominal. A new line begins after the introduction to speech. A subordinate clause with a conjunction is also separated. Elements put in recognizable parallel are separated; however, infinitive constructions such as "in order to" are not. Every member of the predicate can be separated in its function as an adjunct of some kind—coordinating, descriptive, or explicative. Square brackets indicate words added for sense in English; parentheses contain alternative translations or literal renderings.

"God" has been used to translate the Hebrew *ʾElohîm.* "YHWH" in the literal translations is "the LORD" in the NRSV and quotations from it.

In upper case the "Exile," "Exilic," and "post-Exilic" refer to the Israelites' period of deportation to Babylon in the sixth century B.C.E. In lower case the word "exile" means one such person or the condition generally. In upper case "Book" means the Book of Ezra, Nehemiah, or another biblical book. In lower case with reference to Ezra and Nehemiah it means the two of them considered as one unit.

I have used the technical term "Judahite" rather than Israelite or Jewish to indicate the People of the Covenant in the period immediately after the Exile when both the words "Israelite" and "Jew" risk anachronism.

Those who have returned from the Exile are the "remigrants" or the "repatriates." "Returnees" would inaccurately imply a transitive verb.

1:1 In the first year of Cyrus, king of Persia,
[in order] to fulfill the word of YHWH from the
mouth of Jeremiah
YHWH roused the spirit of Cyrus, king of Persia
so that he transmitted a message [lit. "voice"] in
all his kingdom,
and also in writing,
[saying:]

Exordium

1:2 "Thus says Cyrus, king of Persia:
'All the kingdoms of the earth, YHWH the God of
the *heavens has given to me*

Narration

He ordered me to build him a house in Jerusalem
which is in Judah.

Proposition

1:3 Who[ever there is] among you from all his
people,
may his God be with him!
Let him go up to Jerusalem
which is in Judah,
and let him build the house of YHWH, the God
of Israel.
He is the God
who is in Jerusalem.

1:4 And each survivor [lit. "remainder"] from all the
places
where he dwells
let them support him [lit. "lift him up"]
—the men of his place—
with silver
and with gold
and with goods
and with cattle

Conclusion

[together] *with free-will offerings*
for the house of God
which [or who] is in Jerusalem.'"

1:5 The family heads [lit. "the heads of fathers"]
of Judah and Benjamin,
the priests and the Levites

—all [those] whose spirit God had roused—
rose up (prepared?)
to go up
to build the house of Yhwh
which is in Jerusalem.

1:6 And all their neighbors helped [lit. "strengthened
  their hands"]
with vessels of silver,
with the gold,
with the goods,
with the cattle,
with excellent things,
in addition to [lit.: "only on"] what was given
  freely [i.e., as a free-will offering].

Chapter One

EZRA 1:1-6

Introduction

The first six chapters of Ezra are the description of the first return of the Jewish exiles under Zerubbabel and the rebuilding of the Temple. They are a hybrid of imperial decrees, letters, inventories, censuses, and narrative. In them the main characters are introduced and the task of rebuilding is begun. The construction is opposed but the conflict is resolved. At the conclusion the work is completed and the people celebrate the Passover.

The beginning, Ezra 1:1-6, declares that the Exile is over. Cyrus, king of Persia, issues a decree allowing the return of the Jews and soliciting help for them. Those Jews whom YHWH's spirit has roused respond to the king, and all their neighbors help.

Rhetorical Situation

These first verses of Ezra–Nehemiah address a rhetorical issue: how to assimilate change into the people's lives of faithful obedience to YHWH. What must be reconstituted from their pre-exilic society as essential to their Jewishness? How much of their dislocated experience in Babylon is conformable to their belief in YHWH? Above all, how will the new Judah know YHWH's will?

Behind this issue of adaptation is the apparent contradiction between YHWH's promise of freedom in the inherited tradition and the Jews' current subservience to the Persians. The Jewish people were not extinguished in the fall of Judah and the deportations to Babylon; in that sense YHWH's prophecy of salvation in the Exilic prophets has been fulfilled. But how can they now understand their vassalage in Judah as a protraction of that divine grace?[1] "'Behold, we are this day

---

[1] Antonius H. J. Gunneweg, "Zur Interpretation der Bücher Esra–Nehemia: Zugleich ein Beitrag zur Methode der Exegese," *Congress Volume, Vienna, 1980.* VT.S

slaves; [in] the land that you gave to our ancestors in order that we eat its fruit and its good gifts, behold, we are slaves on it'" (Neh 9:36).

The author must show the continuity of the people's history. The YHWH who punished them with Exile is the same who now allows them back. And the period of the Return that begins with this decree is theologically coherent with the author's own time, however many decades after.[2]

The Israelites' history is one whole, despite the disasters, because YHWH is one and consistent, despite his punishments. YHWH rules both in Babylon and in Judah. This desire for continuity would explain the partial repetition of Cyrus's decree at the end of Chronicles (2 Chron 36:22-23) and here. It is a redactional stitch tying the two books together to give a textual dimension to the theological idea. The return of the Temple vessels and the resumption of the old forms of worship (3:3-6) make the same point within the liturgy. At the same time the author must avoid any triumphalism that might lead to complacency or the idea that the messianic age had arrived.[3]

Similarly, Cyrus must be presented as an instrument of YHWH but not his representative, and the passage must also validate the leadership of the family heads, priests, and Levites (v. 5). They are the ones who will carry out the reconstruction.

The fundamental changes this passage examines in the light of faith are the shifts in the authoritative channels of Israel's connectedness with YHWH. Before the Exile YHWH made himself known through the power of the prophets, the kings, the cult, and to some extent already the written text. The author must make clear how YHWH remains sovereign and knowable in new relationships: between the king and YHWH, between the prophetic word and the written text, between the

---

32, ed. J. A. Emerton (Leiden: Brill, 1981) 160; Sara Japhet "Sheshbazzar and Zerubbabel—Against the Background of the Historical and Religious Tendencies of Ezra–Nehemiah," *ZAW* 94 (1982) 75; Celine Mangan, *1–2 Chronicles, Ezra, Nehemiah,* OTMes 13, eds. Carroll Stuhlmueller and Martin McNamara (Wilmington, Del.: Michael Glazier, 1982) li.

[2] The date of composition is controverted. Many scholars would argue that Ezra 1–6 is among the last of the segments, perhaps as late as 300 B.C.E. See, for example, H. G. M. Williamson, *Ezra and Nehemiah* (Sheffield: JSOT Press, 1987) 46, and Mark Throntveit, *Ezra–Nehemiah,* Interpretation, ed. Paul Achtemeier (Louisville: John Knox, 1992) 30. On the other hand, David J. A. Clines, *Ezra, Nehemiah, Esther,* NCBC, eds. Ronald E. Clements and Matthew Black (Grand Rapids: Eerdmans, 1984) 14, believes the whole work was completed by 400 B.C.E., still almost 150 years after the Return itself.

[3] J. G. McConville, *Ezra, Nehemiah, and Esther,* The Daily Study Bible 21, ed. John C. L. Gibson (Philadelphia: Westminster, 1985) 9.

whole community and its leaders. The book treats one of the oldest questions in religion, that of the association between faith and power.

The Speaker and the Audience

The king's remarks are in the mode of persuasion technically called "ethical." We saw in the Introduction that this kind relies for its power to convince on the character and position of the speaker. The king does not use subtle argumentation here. Rather he combines his authority with that of YHWH in ways that are best explained by the introduction of another term.

The decree is a clear example of what is called "performative language," explained in the Introduction. The royal mandate has illocutionary power because the king is ruler. Its perlocutionary power is more subtle: those whose spirits YHWH has roused obey him. The king's authority is not the same as YHWH's, but they are correlated in their effects.

Cyrus calls on the Jews as the children of YHWH with the awkward phrase "who[ever] there is among you from all his people" (v. 3a). They are to rebuild the Temple. The king also wants them supported by "each survivor from all the places where he dwells" (v. 4a). (The word for "survivor," literally "remainder," seems to imply those Jews who had escaped death at the time of the Babylonian attack on Judah in 587/6 and been deported.)[4]

The composition of the audience reflects these rhetorical problems of identity and authority. YHWH is active but silent. That is, he directs the discourse but does not speak himself. Instead, a Persian administrative text transmits YHWH's will by quoting the king who says he is speaking on divine orders: "Thus says Cyrus, king of Persia: '—YHWH the God of the heavens, he ordered me to build him a house . . .'" (v. 2).

---

[4] F. Charles Fensham, *The Books of Ezra and Nehemiah*, NIC, ed. R. K. Harrison (Grand Rapids: Eerdmans, 1982) 44; Clines, *Ezra, Nehemiah, Esther* 38. H. G. M. Williamson, *Ezra, Nehemiah* (Waco, Texas: Word Books, 1985) 14 agrees that the phrase means the Jews who stay in Babylon but he translates it "those who remain behind." Joseph Blenkinsopp, *Ezra–Nehemiah*, OTL, eds. Peter Ackroyd and others (Philadelphia: Westminster, 1988) 75–76, and Joachim Becker, *Esra–Nehemia*, NEB.AT 25, eds. Josef G. Plöger and Josef Schreiner (Würzburg: Echter Verlag, 1990) 16 interpret it as the neighboring Gentiles but admit the historical impossibility. The syntax is made all the more obscure by "the men of the place" (v. 4), perhaps an explanatory gloss in a pedantic judicial style. See the discussion on v. 4 in H. G. M. Williamson, "The Composition of Ezra i–vi" *JThS* n.s. 34 (1983) 9–11, but against him Clines, *Ezra, Nehemiah, Esther* 38.

Before this decree Cyrus has already been roused by YHWH, but Cyrus quotes none of this revelation by which he learned that he must build YHWH a house.

The decree's religious language may be conventional diplomatic diction according to some commentaries.[5] Nonetheless, it has rhetorical and theological implications. The king is the speaker to the Jews, but he has already been a listener to YHWH. And Cyrus's speech itself is not direct but quoted from the writing.

Ezra–Nehemiah is quite unlike the prophetic books where the prophets cry out YHWH's words, beginning "Thus says the LORD."[6] It is of the "deliberative" species. That is, it is intended to bring people to a decision. But here the king is only a puppet of YHWH who is the subject of the opening sentence[7] and, as the prophets know, raises kings and "makes [them] as nothing" (Isa 40:23-24). So in effect the species of the speech is "epideictic." This kind of rhetoric is meant to celebrate a quality or a person, here YHWH. The rhetoric is therefore imperious but also self-attenuating. The mandate is not an obligation to return, but an invitation,[8] and the audience that was initially "all his kingdom" becomes effectively some of the Jews and their neighbors of good will.[9]

The circumscribed quality of YHWH's revelation through Cyrus helps redefine the connection between faith and authority. On YHWH's behalf and to fulfill his word to the prophet Jeremiah the king commissions the reconstitution of the Jerusalem cult but without theophany, wonder, promise, or threat. For all it is divinely inspired and royal, the rhetoric is prosaic in a way that hints at a resolution to the subtle tension between YHWH's freedom and Persian domination. The freedom that YHWH offers now is unlike the furious revolution of the Exodus from Egypt: "Sing of Yahweh; he has covered himself in glory, horse and rider he has thrown into the sea" (Exod 15:21). He will not make them adventurously dependent on him as in the chaotic desert. The Jews will be freed from captivity in Babylon in order to search for the will of YHWH in the mundane events of life. Nor can they find him

---

[5] Referred to in McConville, *Ezra, Nehemiah, and Esther* 7.

[6] Contrast, for example, the very frequent occurence of the phrase in Ezekiel's and Jeremiah's prophecies to Israel.

[7] Antonius H. J. Gunneweg, *Esra*, KAT 19/1 (Gütersloh: Gerd Mohn, 1985) 41.

[8] The Hebrew verbs are in the jussive.

[9] Kurt Galling, "Die Proklamation des Kyros in Esra 1," in idem, *Studien zur Geschichte Israels im persischen Zeitalter* (Tübingen: J. C. B. Mohr [Paul Siebeck], 1964) 66 mentions that Cyrus does not explicitly address all the nations and peoples of his empire as Darius does in Dan 6:26.

now in the majesty of the former Davidic dynasty. His will is done through an administrative document.

The second part of the passage (vv. 5-6) tells of the circumscribed effect of the king's words. Those who respond are "the family heads of Judah and Benjamin, the priests and the Levites—all those whose spirit YHWH had roused" and "all their neighbors" (vv. 5, 6). These references to the diverse audiences resemble the relaying and narrowing of the message itself. God addresses Cyrus "offstage." The king reports those instructions in a decree sent to "all his kingdom," but the Jews alone are affected. From among them we know only of the leaders and the others who have been inspired. Their action then spurs their neighbors' help.

It is YHWH who initiates these responses. He forms the group of enspirited Jews who accepted the invitation of the king, just as he prompted the decree itself. All the subsequent events in Ezra 1:5–Neh 7:72 are thus due to divine initiative,[10] and the failure of some other Jews to return home is covered with a theological excuse.[11] More pertinent to our reading, in ways that we will see, the rhetoric itself inherits something of the prophets' authority, even without their personal flair.

Usually the opening of an address tries to establish the speaker's worth and good will. Here the chief rhetorical task is to define not the speaker but the audience, the people of YHWH. Simply being an exile will no longer suffice.[12] The obedience of one's spirit to YHWH is a condition for participating in the give and take of the rhetoric and, by implication, belonging fully to the people who enjoy his divine company: "Who[ever there is] among you from all his people, may his God be with him! Let him go up to Jerusalem. . . . He is the God who is in Jerusalem" (v. 3).

Moreover, the mass of the people is not defined by its leading citizens only. Although Jeshua and Zerubbabel will emerge as the leaders when the people gather again as one person (Ezra 3:1), the leaders are not the only ones responsible for the rebuilding of the society and its Temple.[13] The "people" here comprise the family heads, the priests and Levites—everyone whose spirit has been roused. And this group is formed before any of its chiefs is named.

---

[10] Tamara Cohn Eskenazi, *In an Age of Prose. A Literary Approach to Ezra–Nehemiah* (Atlanta, Ga.: Scholars, 1988) 46.

[11] Williamson, *Ezra, Nehemiah* 16.

[12] McConville, *Ezra, Nehemiah, and Esther* 10.

[13] Eskenazi, *Age of Prose* 50.

Arrangement

The decree actually does not declare the end of the Exile. It mandates only the rebuilding of the Temple. By its silence about their freedom to move, Ezra–Nehemiah implies that the Jews do not need any persuasion to return to their God-given homeland. The book cannot imply any denigration of the faith of the Jews in Exile since the protagonists, Ezra and Nehemiah, were born and raised there.[14] We have seen how obedience to YHWH is the criterion of the intended audience. The call for faithfulness also shapes the rhetoric itself.

EXORDIUM (V. 2A-C)

Despite its bureaucratic origin and written form the decree follows the various steps often seen in oral rhetoric. In this way it is unique in Ezra–Nehemiah. The rhetorical terms are classical Latin, but the realities are not tied to that culture. The opening section of a persuasive communication normally seeks the attention and good will of the audience. It shows why one should take the position to be explained. Emphasis is on the qualities that the audience may doubt.[15]

Cyrus does not need flattery or ornament here. He is incontrovertible: he simply says he has been commissioned by God who has already given him all the kingdoms of the earth. The plainest reality in the rhetorical situation is that he has power. We read twice in as many verses that he is the "king of Persia" (vv. 1c, 2a). He shows no further need for winning the favor of the audience by proving his assertion, because he can command their attention.

Since both Ezra and Nehemiah are presented as working under the direct orders of the Persians, the interest of the book lies in showing first that YHWH directs the Persians.[16]

NARRATIO (V. 2D-E)

The function of this section is normally to set forth the information that prompts the rhetoric. Here rather than facts we have assertions.

---

[14] Throntveit, *Ezra–Nehemiah* 16.

[15] George A. Kennedy, *New Testament Interpretation through Rhetorical Criticism* (Chapel Hill and London: University of North Carolina Press, 1984) 48; Chaïm Perelman and Lucie Olbrechts-Tyteca, *Traité de l'argumentation: La nouvelle rhétorique* (5th ed. Brussels: Editions de l'Université de Bruxelles, 1988; original publication 1958) 657, 659.

[16] Mangan, *1–2 Chronicles, Ezra, Nehemiah* 163.

The persuasiveness of the section comes from the authority of the speaker, Cyrus. His certain political power strengthens his unprovable theological claim that YHWH revealed his will to him.

PROPOSITIO (VV. 3A-4I)

After the background information in the *narratio* a piece of rhetoric will often naturally set out its proposition—the action or decision that the speaker entreats of the audience. Here it is proposed that the Jews return to Jerusalem with the help of their neighbors and set about rebuilding the Temple.

Ancient rhetoricians thought such a section could be brief, complete and concise.[17] The whole decree is so.

Strikingly, there is no attempt to set out common ground with the audience or prove the point to them.[18] The king does not offer arguments for his proposition. None is given here because none is called for. YHWH is always free to act without self-justification. Nor does an autocrat need to explain why he is issuing a decree, especially since we already know that YHWH has prompted him. Cyrus and, through him, YHWH never make clear why the Temple is needed in Jerusalem again. To attempt to prove the point would weaken it as a axiom of faith.

Instead of logical proof that the Jews should go to Jerusalem the king's speech uses force of repetition to bring together the city, the Jews, the Temple, and YHWH. Repetition is a rhetorical tool often used in communication in the "ethical" mode. He exclaims: "Who[ever there is] among you from all his people, may his God be with him!" This was apparently a pagan greeting already absorbed into Jewish conversation and put by the author of Ezra–Nehemiah into the mouth of the Persian king,[19] but the salutation takes on persuasive effect when used with a repeated phrase. Four times the decree ponderously spells out: "a house in Jerusalem, which is in Judah. . . . Let him go up to

---

[17] Hans Dieter Betz, *Galatians: A Commentary on Paul's Letter to the Churches in Galatia.* Hermeneia, eds. Frank Moore Cross, Helmut Koester, et al. (Philadelphia: Fortress, 1979) 114 n. 12, citing Cicero and Quintilian.

[18] When rhetoric does so the section is called the "probatio" and it follows the "narratio." See Betz, *Galatians* 114; Hans Dieter Betz, *2 Corinthians 8 and 9 : A Commentary on Two Administrative Letters of the Apostle Paul*, ed. George W. MacRae. Hermeneia (Philadelphia: Fortress, 1985) 100–101.

[19] Williamson, *Ezra, Nehemiah* 13, citing E. J. Bickerman, "The Edict of Cyrus in Ezra 1," *Studies in Jewish and Christian History* 1 (Leiden: Brill, 1976) 72–108, and R. A. Bowman, "Introduction and Exegesis to the Book of Ezra and the Book of Nehemiah," *IB* 3:552–819. See also 2 Chron 36:23.

Jerusalem which is in Judah. . . . He is the God who is in Jerusalem . . .
the House of God which [or who] is in Jerusalem." Such pedantic
specificity is official style,[20] but its concentrated and frequent use here
creates an association of realities.

Cyrus also concludes the decree with the ambiguous "the house of
YHWH which [or who] is in Jerusalem,"[21] and for good measure he
gives the double title "YHWH, the God of Israel."

The combined implication of all these modifying phrases and
clauses is that for a Jew to be with YHWH he or she should go to Jerusalem in Israel to the Temple that is YHWH's house. It is a line of
thought founded, not on strict argument, but on the created sense of
what is real, on what one scholar of rhetoric calls the "aptness of consequences."[22] The God-given insight and authority of Cyrus add so-
lidity to the reality projected by the repetitious detail, that God wants
the Jews in Jerusalem worshiping him in his Temple there.

The author would not want to make the point more sharply than
he does because YHWH is not in Jerusalem only. He is also with the Persian king whom he inspired to free the Jews in the first place. And
Cyrus universalizes YHWH as the god of all the heavens.

Not surprisingly for the decree of an autocrat, this one has no rhetorically distinct conclusion. An address often closes by trying to
sharpen the main points of the case, to arouse anger and hostility
against the opponents and to stimulate pity.[23] But the king's majesty
does not admit of any opponents, and sentiment is beneath him.

Stylistic Devices

The Return from Exile announced here is described in terms that allude to the escape from Egypt. "To bring up . . . from [a place] to [a
place]" in Ezra 1:11 recalls the same expression about the Exodus in

---

[20] Fensham, *Books of Ezra–Nehemiah* 43–44; Clines, *Ezra, Nehemiah, Esther* 37–38;
Williamson, *Ezra, Nehemiah* 12, citing L. V. Hensley, *The Official Persian Documents in
the Book of Ezra*, University of Liverpool. (Unpublished dissertation 1977). Repetition as a rhetorical device is called "epimone" and is considered the most important means of making associations, according to Heinrich Lausberg, *Handbuch der
literarischen Rhetorik: Eine Grundlegung der Literaturwissenschaft* (3rd ed. Stuttgart:
Franz Steiner, 1990; original publication 1960) 1:125.

[21] On the ambiguous antecedent of the Hebrew relative pronoun see Blenkinsopp, *Ezra–Nehemiah* 75.

[22] Lausberg, *Handbuch* 1:198.

[23] Betz, *Galatians* 313.

Exod 33:1; 3:8, 17; Gen 50:24. The gold, silver, goods, and beasts offered to the repatriates are like the treasures despoiled from the Egyptians by the Hebrews in Exod 3:21-22; 11:2; 12:35-36; Ps 105:37.

No response is made to the version of the decree in Chronicles and it says nothing of those who stay behind. Repetition is often used in an "ethical" mode of rhetoric, as here. Thus to amplify the effect of the decree here, the people's reception of it is given in many ways as its echo.

King's Decree	*Description of People's Response*
YHWH roused the spirit of Cyrus . . . (v. 1)	—all [those] whose spirit God had roused—rose up . . . (v. 5)
"Let him go up to Jerusalem . . . and let him build the house of YHWH. . . . He is the god who is in Jerusalem (v. 3).	[They] rose up (prepared?) to go up to build the house of YHWH which is in Jerusalem (v. 5).
"Let them support him [lit. lift him up]" (v. 4)	[They] rose up (prepared?) to go up . . . (v. 5)
"with silver and with gold and with goods and with cattle [together] with free-will offerings" (v. 4)	with vessels of silver, with the gold, with the goods, with the cattle, with excellent things, in addition to what was given freely (v. 6)

The description of the people's response repeats the king's call to them, just as the decree repeats its own phrases. This internal and external antiphony is like the style of the account of creation in Genesis 1. Compare: "God said, 'Let there be light'; and there was light. . . . And God said, 'Let there be a dome in the midst of the waters, and let it separate the waters from the waters.' So God made the dome and separated the waters that were under the dome from the waters that were above the dome" (Gen 1:4, 6). This similarity of style hints at Ezra 1's association with Second Isaiah's promise that the Return is to be a new creation as well as a new Exodus.

"I, the LORD, am first, and will be with the last" (Isa 41:4).

"Do not remember the former things, or consider the things of old. I am about to do a new thing; now it springs forth, do you not perceive it?" (Isa 43:18-19).

". . . remember the former things of old . . . I am God, and there is no one like me, declaring the end from the beginning and from ancient times things not yet done. . . . I have spoken, and I will bring it to pass; I have planned, and I will do it" (Isa 46:9-11).

Beyond the creation motif Isa 45:12-13 is a particularly striking parallel of theme and vocabulary:

I made the earth, and created humankind upon it;
it was my hands that stretched out the heavens,
and I commanded all their host.
I have aroused [Cyrus] in righteousness,
and I will make all his paths straight;
he shall build my city
and set my exiles free . . .

(Other references to "rousing" and to Cyrus are in Isa 41:2, 25; 44:28; 45:1.)

The decree is "in order to fulfill the word of YHWH from the mouth of Jeremiah" (v. 1). Given the evident allusions to Second Isaiah, it may be that the text speaks of Jeremiah here because of Jeremiah 51 where YHWH promises to "rouse the spirit of a destroyer against Babylon." The intertextual mesh of Ezra, Second Isaiah, and Jeremiah here implies that Cyrus the Persian was empowered by YHWH to destroy Babylon in order to free the Jews to return home.[24]

The allusions to the Exodus, to the prophets, and through them to the Pentateuch are subtle because the author wants in no way to imply that Cyrus is equal to Moses, Isaiah, or Jeremiah. Still, they work to present the consistency between the present day and God's salvific history. We saw how that is part of the rhetorical situation: the author seeks to show the unbroken possibility of faithful life despite the change in the channels of God's word and the nature of national authority.

Conclusions

To promote this hopefulness in the face of change the passage has set out three new relations that mark Israel's faith life.

---

[24] So Williamson, *Ezra, Nehemiah* 10.

The King and Yhwh

Although a foreigner, Cyrus is Yhwh's agent but not his image or his punishing instrument.

The Word and the Text

In Israel's faith the written text begins to supercede the oral and prophetic word that nevertheless still obtains as a source of inspiration and understanding.

Israel and Yhwh

Third, the community itself begins to be redefined not by mere birth but by its spirit-filled responsiveness to Yhwh's communication through the text

With these themes the opening four verses of Ezra anticipate the whole of Ezra–Nehemiah. The assertions of Israel's creed hold true after the Exile, as before and during it—Yhwh's almightiness, his self-communication, and the community he wills. What has changed with circumstances is the relationship of that perduring faith to the credentials and message of its interpreters.

The passage rhetorically persuades the Jews and the readers of whatever era that to assimilate change one must first rediscover the unchangeable. Here that essential reality is faithfulness to Yhwh. It then becomes the criterion to define the rightful direction for reform and the fitting agent to promote it.

EZRA 4:1-24 — LITERAL TRANSLATION

4:1   The adversaries of Judah and Benjamin heard
that the children of the exile were building a palace for YHWH
    the God of Israel.

4:2   They approached Zerubbabel and the heads of fathers' houses
and said to them,
"Let us build with you;
for, as you do, we consult your God.
And to him we have been sacrificing
since the days of Esar-haddon king of Assyria
who brought us up here.

4:3   Zerubbabel, Jeshua, and the rest of the heads of father's houses
    of Israel said to them
"It is not up to you but to us to build a house to our God
for we alone will build for YHWH the God of Israel,
as King Cyrus the king of Persia has commanded us."

4:4   Then the people of the land discouraged [lit. "weakened the
    hands of"] the people of Judah
and made trouble for them in building [or: made them afraid to
    build].

4:5   They hired counsellors against them to frustrate their counsel
even until the reign of Darius king of Persia.

4:6   And in the reign of Ahasuerus,
in the beginning of his reign,
they wrote an accusation against the inhabitants of Judah and
Jerusalem.

4:7   And in the days of Artaxerxes,
Bishlam and Mithredath and Tabeel and the rest of their associates
wrote to Artaxerxes, king of Persia;
the letter was written in Aramaic and interpreted in Aramaic.

4:8   Rehum the chancellor and Shimshai the scribe wrote a letter
    concerning [lit. "against"] Jerusalem to Artaxerxes
as follows:

4:9   then Rehum the chancellor, Shimshai the scribe, and the rest of
    their associates, the judges, the officials, the men of Tarpel,
    Sippar, Erech, Babylon, Susa (that is, Elam),

4:10   and the rest of the peoples
whom the great and noble Osnappar deported
and settled
in the cities [lit. "city"] of Samaria and in the rest of the province
    Beyond the River

14

and now

4:11   this is a copy of the letter that they sent:

"To Artaxerxes the king:

Your servants,

the men of the province Beyond the River,

send [greetings]

and now,

4:12   be it known to the king

that the Jews

who came up from you [lit. "your side"] to us

have gone to Jerusalem.

They are rebuilding that rebellious and wicked city;

they are finishing [surveying?; beginning to finish?] the walls

and repairing the foundations.

4:13   Now be it known to the king

that

if this city is rebuilt

and the walls finished

they will not pay tribute, custom, or poll tax,

and the royal interests [revenues?] will finally [or: certainly?]
    be impaired.

4:14   Now because we eat the salt of the palace

and it is not fitting for us

to witness the king's dishonor;

therefore we send [word]

and inform the king,

4:15   in order that search may be made in the book of the records of
    your predecessors [lit. "fathers"].

You (lit. "he") will find in the book of the records

and learn

that this city is a rebellious city,

hurtful to kings and provinces,

and that sedition was stirred up in it from ancient times.

That is why this city was laid waste.

4:16   We make it known to the king

that

if this city is rebuilt

and its walls finished,

you will then have no tax revenue in the province Beyond
    the River."

4:17   The king sent an answer:

"To Rehum the chancellor and Shimshai the scribe and the rest
    of their associates

who live in Samaria and in the rest of the province Beyond the
    River,
peace!
And now

4:18   the letter
which you sent to us
has been plainly read before me.

4:19   And I made the decree,
and search has been made,
and it has been found
that this city from of old has risen against kings
and that rebellion and sedition have been made in it.

4:20   And mighty kings have been over Jerusalem,
and exercised authority over the whole province Beyond the
    River,
to whom tribute, custom, and poll-tax were paid.

4:21   Now then make a decree
that these men be made to cease,
and that this city not be rebuilt,
until a decree is made by me.

4:22   And be warned not to be negligent in this matter
lest the damage grow to the injury of the king(s?)."

4:23   Then, when the copy of King Artaxerxes' letter was read before
    Rehum and Shimshai the scribe and their associates,
they went in haste to the Jews at Jerusalem
and by main strength and arms made them cease.

4:24   Then [?] ceased the work on the house of God
which is in Jerusalem;
and it ceased until the second year of the reign of Darius, king
    of Persia.

Chapter Two
EZRA 4:1-24

Introduction

The last passage we examined, Ezra 1:1-6, sets in motion the rhetorical machine of the entire book. Subsequent to it the treasure of the Jerusalem Temple is counted and handed over to Sheshbazzar, the leader of Judah (1:8). In ch. 2 the "households" or clans of those who return and their number and status are listed. The image is of all the leaders of Israel returning with the cultic objects, as if in a liturgical procession. The Israelites gather together, literally "as one man," to set the altar up again (3:1). They celebrate the Festival of Booths despite their fear of the people of the land. As permitted by the king, they go about laying the foundations of the new Temple. In 3:11 the narrator reaffirms the eternal love of YHWH for his people.

By the time they have returned to Israel the chief Sheshbazzar has disappeared and been replaced without explanation by Zerubbabel. It is as though his existence depends on, and is circumscribed by, his task in the story, and that function is to return the cultic objects. In a book full of genealogies Sheshbazzar has none. Even his father's name is unmentioned. In his turn Zerubbabel will leave the story without explanation once the Temple is finally complete.

This switch in leadership is the most obvious of the many puzzles in Ezra 4 that have largely absorbed scholars' attention. Other incongruities and overlaps complicate the plot, and most of the statistics are unlikely.

No one is sure who "the people of the land" were.[1] They may or may not be ancestors of the Samaritans of the New Testament. In Haggai

---

[1] They may have been descended from foreign intellectuals and bureaucrats brought into the Northern Kingdom by Assyria to administer the territory. They may have been the landholders who had formerly been disenfranchised, or some of the Samaritan upper class, or a "fifth column" previously supported by Jeremiah

1:1-10 the blame for delay in reestablishing the Law is laid on the repatriates themselves for being lazy and selfish. Here, as we will see, it is these "people of the land" who are guilty.

Despite obstacles the Judahites toil to restore their cult. They offer sacrifices. They lay the foundations of the Temple. Just before the passage to be studied now they shout with joy at the sight of the restoration work. Ambiguously, some older individuals remember the earlier Temple and weep. By a neat verbal stitch ch. 3 is tied to ch. 4: the shouting of the people is "heard"; then the adversaries "hear" of the Temple construction.

Rhetorical Situation

In 1:1-6, the first discourse we examined, the rhetorical situation was the dual need to affirm the consistency of YHWH in the Judahites' history and yet to promote the adaptability of their faith. YHWH is powerfully present in a new matrix of associations between divine and imperial sovereignty, between the written and the oral word, between the people and the leaders.

Here the situation builds on the points already established about the nature of authority: the Persian king is divinely sanctioned and the Judahites' leaders may speak for the whole community.

The reader of Ezra 4 is puzzled by the silences of the text. From the beginning the narrator calls the people of the land "adversaries" of the Judahites. We learn in 3:3 that the repatriates are afraid of them. We are not told the reason. Why may they not participate in the rebuilding of the Temple? (The king commissioned the repatriates, but he did not forbid others to help.) Why do the people want to stop the work simply because they may not help in it? A rhetorical analysis can help resolve these points of curiosity.

The Judahites say little here. The rhetoric is chiefly in the exchange of letters between the people of the land and the king. The Judahite leaders say only that the people of the land may not participate in the rebuilding of the Temple. The people must then persuade the king to stop its construction, but they must bring him to change his predeces-

---

and Gedaliah, or former debtors and even slaves. For the first theory see Bruce C. Birch, *Let Justice Roll Down: The Old Testament, Ethics and Christian Life* (Louisville: Westminster/John Knox, 1991) 309. For the others see Daniel L. Smith, *The Religion of the Landless: The Social Context of the Babylonian Exile* (Bloomington, Ind.: Meyer-Stone Books, 1989) 196.

sor's decision without criticizing it. The crisis is the need of the people of the land to establish a place for themselves in the new Judahite society following the Return of the repatriates. For their part the repatriates circumscribe the adaptability of their faith by excluding others from it. In doing so they test their self-sufficiency in their weakened and subordinate state.

In time Ezra will proclaim the Law to them and apprise them of the content of their faith. In Ezra–Nehemiah, however, before doctrine can be embraced community must be built. And the community of the Judahites will be built around the common project of the Temple's construction.

Rhetorical Audience: the Letter-Writers and Letter-Readers

Only these two groups exist for the author. The text begins by assuming the equation of the "sons of the Exiles" and "Judah and Benjamin," then contrasting them to the people of the land as their adversaries: "When the adversaries of Judah and Benjamin heard that the returned exiles were building a temple to the LORD, the God of Israel . . . then the people of the land discouraged the people of Judah . . ." (4:1, 4). Any member of the authentic Judean community is called literally a "son of the Exile." The mixed "people of the land" is in the singular only here in Ezra–Nehemiah, as though they stood united.[2]

Although this "people of the land" is victorious in the first analysis the text on another level diminishes them in favor of the protagonists, the Judahites. Their letter persuades the king to stop the project, but its arguments discredit the writers in our eyes. In ways we will see, their attack gives value to their own opponents, the Judahites.

The first observation is that the identity of the writers is unclear. Their names are detailed, but confused. Perhaps an irregularity in the transmission of the text has resulted in the combination of two letters under two Persian kings signed by people whose names vary. Did they write "in the beginning of the reign of Ahasuerus" (v. 6) or "in the days of Artaxerxes" (v. 7)? Are Bishlam, Mithredath, Tabeel, and "the rest of the associates" (v. 7) the same group as in v. 9—Rehum the chancellor, Shimshai the scribe, and the rest of their associates listed by rank and

---

[2] Sara Japhet, "'History' and 'Literature' in the Persian Period: The Restoration of the Temple," in *Ah, Assyria . . . Studies in Assyrian History and Ancient Near Eastern Historiography Presented to Hayim Tadmor*, eds. Mordechai Cogan and Israel Eph'al (Jerusalem: Magnes Press, 1991) 180. The phrase "people of the land" is the opposite of the meaning in Hag 2:4 and Zech 7:5.

nationality including all the nations deported by the Assyrians? For Baruch Halpern the switch in dating from the regnal year to the year after the Return, after ch. 1, and back again in ch. 4 suggests that the ambiguity is deliberate.[3]

Text criticism and historical criticism make valuable hypotheses along their own lines. But interpreting the text as it comes to us, rhetorical criticism sees the effect of such confusion. The enemy, the people of the land, is strong but without identity while the Judahites are weak but self-reliant. One effect is that the leaders of the people are too blurred to gain prestige in our sight despite their successful association with the ruler. And a king whose very name is unclear can scarcely supersede YHWH's ultimate authority although in Ezra–Nehemiah YHWH is nowhere overtly active.

The rhetorical constraint on the petition-writers is that they may not criticize the mandate to rebuild the Temple, although they want it reversed. And they cannot expect the king to have any interest in their desire to find their place in the new post-Exilic society of Judah.

Rhetorical Strategies

The Temple is treated here as a synecdoche, a rhetorical figure in which a part represents the whole. That is, the Temple stands for the whole of the relationship between YHWH and the Judahites.

The strategies to develop this relation build on a point of unclarity in ch. 1. The king said that YHWH had ordered him to build the Temple. He does not build it himself, of course, but orders the Judahites to do so. They are the hands of the king in performing YHWH's will in a way that YHWH did not explicitly order or forbid. They now expand their role in this divine mandate.

The narration in v. 1 sets the stage by calling the people of the land "the adversaries of Judah and Benjamin" and YHWH "the God of Israel" (v. 1). The words placed in the mouth of the people of the land admit their religious dependence on the children of the Exile: they ask to help build the Temple because, they say, they "consult your God," that is, the exiles'. The Judahites can then simply claim the fullness of this superior connection to YHWH, using the titles for him already given by the narrator and the people: "It is not up to you but to us to

[3] Baruch Halpern, "A Historiographic Commentary on Ezra 1–6: Achronological Narrative and Dual Chronology in Israelite Historiography," *The Hebrew Bible and its Interpreters*, eds. William H. Propp, Baruch Halpern, and David N. Freedman. Biblical and Judaic Studies 1 (Winona Lake, Ind.: Eisenbrauns, 1990) 110.

build a house to *our God*; for we alone will build for YHWH *the God of Israel.*" The language and the plot of the chapter deepen the "ethos" or relationship with YHWH that the Judahites enjoy and that enhances them in our eyes. In the Introduction, we saw that one of the fundamental modes of rhetoric is built on "ethos."

The people of the land, on the other hand, seek an advantageous rhetorical association with the king. In rhetoric, an approach that builds on the bond between the communicator and the hearer is called "ethical." It is founded on the "ethos" of the communicator, that is, his or her good sense, good character, and good will. However, the rhetorical ways in which the people of the land show their loyalty and win the king's ear diminish them in our perspective. The argument by ethos works for one audience, the king, but not for the other audience, us.

The species of rhetoric here is deliberative or political, urging action in the future. The chief medium is an exchange of administrative letters, and this fact shapes much of the strategy.

After the introductory narrative the people of the land write to the king. Unlike many other examples of deliberative rhetoric, including the passage studied in ch. 1, no particular attempt is made initially to win the good regard of the other by flattery or obsequiousness. ("Your servants" is a standard Semitic replacement for the first person plural.) Rather than flatter the king with emotional language their petition sets about establishing a liaison with him that represents reality from the angle of the writers. The Return is described as though the writers and the king personally formed the two termini: the Judahites "came up from you [lit. "your side"] to us" (v. 12c), then went on to Jerusalem. In fact the edict of Cyrus mentions nothing about going to the people of the land, only to Jerusalem.

Verses 12 and 13 present an informal syllogism, technically called an enthymeme:

- (Jerusalem has always been rebellious.)
- They are rebuilding Jerusalem.
- Jerusalem will be rebellious again.

An enthymeme is not strictly logical. It seeks to move from what is already accepted by the listener (but unproved, and therefore placed in parentheses) to the conclusion proposed by the communicator. It is based on probability or a reserve of opinions, values, attitudes, and conventions.[4] That the city has always been rebellious is just one

---

[4] See Timothy A. Lenchak, *"Choose Life!" A Rhetorical-Critical Investigation of Deuteronomy 28,69–30,20.* AnBib 129 (Rome: Pontifical Biblical Institute, 1993) 147 n. 80, and the further references cited there.

interpretation of history. It is not strictly logical that the city would refuse to pay taxes in the future even if it had been rebellious in the past, especially in the current straits of the repatriates. Even the middle term is exaggerated: the Judahites have so far been rebuilding the Temple, not the walls of Jerusalem.[5] The enthymeme hangs on the strength of the ethos of trust between the petitioners and the king.

That is why they emphasize the status and favor they enjoy with the king: they have eaten the salt of his palace.[6] Rejected by the Judahites, the people of the land seek a "community of values" with the king. They want their compatibility with the Persian ruler to hold sway over the incompatibility claimed by the Judahites between the people of the land and them: "'It is not up to you but to us to build a house to our God'" (Ezra 4:3).

The petitioners further promote their rhetorical association with the king by referring him to the documented past. The historical record is offered as a predictor of the future. The point in itself is weak. The circumstances of the Judahites are now quite different, and any past glory of Jerusalem could be all the more reason to reconstruct the city for the greater lustre of the Persian Empire to which it now belongs. The petitioners are hoping that their liaison with the king will mask their argument's flawed association between the past and the future, and to enhance this historical argument, they send the king to his own archives. The king will hardly criticize the authority of his own records, making it all the easier to establish the petitioners' questionable point that the documents indicate future action.

They win their case and block the project of the repatriates. The king's response is what the petitioners wanted to hear. But again a closer reading shows that, despite itself, the king's decree gives merit to the Judahites although it censures them. The king is led to admit that the former rulers of Jerusalem were mighty, rich, and proud "from

---

[5] Halpern, "A Historiographic Commentary on Ezra 1–6" 110 gives a historical-critical analysis for the anomalous mention of the wall here. Verses 6-23 would be the story of the interference in work on the wall of Jerusalem at a much later time, in the reigns of Ahasuerus and Artaxerxes. The main story is resumed in 4:24 by a reprise or "epanalepsis" linking it to 4:5: "until the reign of Darius king of Persia." The argumentative effect of the incoherence stands, as does the question why the text was not altered to fit more perfectly when some redactional roughnesses elsewhere are vigorously smoothed over.

[6] By analogy with the Israelite practice (Lev 2:13; Num 18:19; 2 Chron 13:5) the expression may refer to an oath of allegiance as imperial officers, ratified by eating a dish flavored with salt, a precious commodity. See, for example, Joseph Blenkinsopp, *Ezra–Nehemiah* (Philadelphia: Westminster, 1988) 114; H. G. M. Williamson, *Ezra, Nehemiah* (Waco, Texas: Word Books, 1985) 56.

of old" (v. 19). The royal caution is a compliment to the antiquity and prowess of the Judahites' ancestors.

The plot describes a setback for the Judahites, but narration and the rhetorical strategies, even of their enemies, give them greater stature in our eyes. The rhetoric already anticipates the repatriates' eventual resurgence.

The royal letter has illocutionary power or authority because the king is ruler. We know it has perlocutionary power or effectiveness because the people of the land act on it and stop the reconstruction.[7] The people of the land built their case on their good standing with the king, and the king replied by using his royal prerogative. But the description and the language undercut the temporary victors, the Judahites' opponents. In other words Israel's true identity, the issue at stake, is not dependent on human power or relations. The rhetoric is intimating something to be clarified later about the holy nature of the reconstituted Israel.

Stylistic Devices

A number of details reinforce the chapter's attention to the matter of identity in general and the Judahites' in particular. As the conflict grows between them and the people of the land, so does the vocabulary they share. The "people" of the land discourage the "people" of Judah and they set "counsellors" to frustrate their "counsel" (vv. 4-5). The Judahite leaders or "heads of fathers' houses" (v. 2) are stymied by the record of the king's "fathers" or predecessors (v. 15). Since they cannot help build a "palace for YHWH" (v. 1) the petitioners write the king, the salt of whose "palace" they have eaten (v. 14). We saw earlier how the Judahites claim their affiliation to YHWH, using the titles for him already given by the narrator and the people. The shared vocabulary is a stylistic foil for the estrangement of the two camps. Again language acts subversively, just as does the victory of the people of the land against the Judahites, which is described in words that belittle the victors.

In vv. 9-10 the narrator introduces the people of the land in a detailed mixture of name, rank, nationality, and history: "Rehum the chancellor, Shimshai the scribe, and the rest of their associates, the judges, the commissioners, the officials, the Persians, the men of Erech, the Babylonians, the men of Susa, that is, the Elamites, and the rest of the nations whom the great and noble Osnappar deported." (Scholars

---

[7] See the Introduction for the terms perlocutionary and illocutionary power.

differ about the best translation of various nouns.) In a chapter about national identity the list brings out the foreignness of the people of the land. Its effect on us is to underscore the textual and historical confusion already mentioned concerning the background of these people and the date of their correspondence. By contrast the Judahites' identity is promoted by the decisiveness of their own action.

Conclusion

YHWH's self-eclipse here is the counterpoint to the king's autocracy. Since YHWH is silent, we do not know that the king's obstruction of the rebuilding is not somehow still in accord with the divine will.

In the first chapter we saw how Ezra 1:1-6 spoke to the relations between the Judahites and YHWH. It promised the repatriates that they could know YHWH even in the upset of the Return. With that assurance of divine support they now establish their independent identity vis-à-vis the people of the land. They act in faith, as Ezra 1 showed them they could. With Yahwism no longer attached to boundaries and Yahwists all over the Near East, Judean Yahwists had to think of new ways for thinking about eligibility and participation in the Temple system.[8]

The refusal of the language to give rhetorical victory to the victors means that words remain powerful in ways that cannot be controlled politically. Ezra 1:1 announced that what follows is true to the prophet Jeremiah. Language is still a force in this period of the Return, but neither words nor political deeds are true enough to be the center of Israel's new life. The stage is set for the next chapter.

---

[8] David L. Petersen, ed., *The Temple in Persian Period Prophetic Texts.* Second Temple Studies: I. Persian Period. (Sheffield: JSOT Press, 1991) 142.

5:1   Now the prophets Haggai and Zechariah, son of Iddo,
        prophesied to (or against) the Jews
who were in Judah and Jerusalem
in the name of the God of Israel
who was over them.

5:2   Then Zerubbabel, son of Shealtiel, and Jeshua, son of
        Jozadak, set about beginning to build the house of God
        in Jerusalem.
With them were the prophets of God, supporting them.

5:3   At that time Tattenai, pasha of Beyond-the-River, and
        Shethar-bozenai and their associates came to them,
and they spoke to them
thus:
"Who gave you a decree to build this house and to complete
    [the preparation of] this material?"

5:4   They (lit. "we") also asked them this,
"What are the names of the men
who are building this building?"

5:5   But the eye of their God was upon the elders of the Jews
and they did make them cease
while (before?) a report was dispatched,
and then answer was returned by letter concerning this.

5:6   The copy of the letter
which Tattenai, pasha of Beyond-the-River, and Shethar-
        bozenai and his associates, the pashas
who were in the province of Beyond-the-River
sent to Darius, the king:

5:7   They sent him word
and in it there was written
as follows:
"To King Darius, all peace.

5:8   Be it known to the king
that we went to the province of Judah
to the house of the great God.
It is being built with dressed(?) stone
with timber set in the walls.
This work goes on diligently
and prospers in their hands.

5:9   Then we asked of those elders
and spoke to them thus:

'Who gave you a decree to build this house
and to complete [the preparation of] this material?'

5:10   Moreover, we asked them their names
in order that we might inform you;
what we are writing is the names of the men at their head.

5:11   And this was their letter in reply:
'We are the slaves of the God of heaven and earth
and we are building the house
which was built many years ago
which a great king of Israel built and finished.

5:12   But because our fathers angered the God of heaven,
he gave them into the hand of Nebuchadnezzar, king of
        Babylon, the Chaldean;
he both destroyed this house
and exiled the people to Babylon.

5:13   However, in the first year of Cyrus, king of Babylon,
King Cyrus made a decree
that this house of God be built.

5:14   Furthermore, the gold and silver vessels of the house of God
which Nebuchadnezzar had removed from the temple
        in Jerusalem
and brought to the temple in Babylon,
these Cyrus the king took out of the temple of Babylon,
and they were delivered to one whose name was Sheshbazzar,
whom he had made pasha.

5:15   And he said to him,
"Carry these vessels, go
and put them in the temple
which is in Jerusalem,
and let the house of God be built on the site."

5:16   Then this Sheshbazzar came
and laid the foundations of the house of God
which is in Jerusalem.
From then to now, it has been under construction (lit. "in
        building"),
but it is not finished.'

5:17   Therefore, if it seems good to the king,
let search be made in the treasure house of the king, there in
        Babylon to see
whether it really is so
that King Cyrus issued a decree for the building of this
        house of God in Jerusalem.
And let the king send us his pleasure in this matter."

6:1   Then Darius the king made a decree
        and they searched in the house of the archives there in
              Babylon
        where the treasures were stored.
6:2   But in Ecbatana, in the fortress
        which is in the province of Media,
        a scroll was found
        on which was written thus:
        "Memorandum:
6:3   In the first year of Cyrus the king,
        Cyrus the king issued a decree:
        The house of God in Jerusalem
        Let the house be built,
        the place where sacrifices are offered
        and burnt offerings are brought (or: its foundations retained?);
        its height shall be sixty cubits, and its breadth sixty cubits.
6:4   Three rows of dressed stones and a row of new (?) timber;
        let the expenses come from the house of the king.
6:5   And also let the gold and silver vessels of the house of God,
        which Nebuchadnezzar took out of the temple
        that is in Jerusalem
        and brought to Babylon
        be returned
        and brought to the temple
        which is in Jerusalem,
        each to its place;
        you shall deposit them in the house of God."
6:6   "Now, Tattenai, pasha of the province of Beyond-the-River,
              Shethar-bozenai and [you] their associates the inspectors
        who are in the province of Beyond-the-River,
        keep away from there!
6:7   Leave the work on this house of God alone;
        let the pasha of the Jews and the elders of the Jews build this
              house of God on its site.
6:8   Herewith I make a decree regarding
        what you shall do for (lit. "with") these elders of the Jews for
              building of this house of God:
        from the goods of the king, the tribute of the province of
              Beyond-the-River,
        the cost is to be paid to these men completely and
              without delay.
6:9   And whatever is needed—bullocks, rams, or sheep for burnt
              offerings to the God of heaven, wheat, salt, wine, or oil,

according to the command of the priests who are in Jerusalem—let that be given to them day by day without fail,

6:10　so that they may offer pleasing sacrifices to the God of heaven,
and pray for the life of the king and his sons.

6:11　Also I make a decree that
if anyone violates (alters?) this order,
a beam shall be pulled out of his house,
and, fastened erect to it,
he shall be flogged (impaled?)
and his house shall be made into a dunghill (?) for this.

6:12　May the God
who has caused his name to dwell there
overthrow any king or people
who shall put forth a hand to disobey this,
or to destroy this house of God
which is in Jerusalem.
I, Darius, make a decree;
let it be done diligently."

6:13　Then Tattenai the pasha of Beyond-the-River, Shethar-bozenai,
and their associates did diligently
what Darius the king had ordered.

6:14　The elders of the Jews built
and prospered
through the prophesying of Haggai the prophet and of
Zechariah the son of Iddo.
They finished their building
by command of the God of Israel and by the decree of Cyrus
and Darius and Artaxerxes, king of Persia;

6:15　and this house was finished on the third day of the month of
Adar, in the sixth year of the reign of Darius the king.

Chapter Three
EZRA 5:1–6:15

Introduction

In chapter 4 the Judahites refused the help of the neighboring people. They stood up for their solidarity and self-sufficiency. An exchange of documents ended climactically with the work of reconstruction halted by imperial order. The impasse is not resolved, but rather dissolves in chs. 5–6 as an alternative set of correspondence seals the triumph of the Judahites.

This rhetorical exchange in 5–6 comes almost immediately after the previous one. The separation in time is rendered ambiguous and this episode is made to seem the smooth sequel: "[The work] stopped until the second year of Darius, king of Persia. Now the prophets Haggai and Zechariah, son of Iddo, prophesied . . ." (4:24–5:1).

Background realities have suddenly changed. Two new figures, the prophets Haggai and Zechariah, inspire the people to the task of reconstruction as though no enemies or imperial decree impeded them. Indeed, the Judahites write that the construction has been going on since the foundations were laid (5:16). Zerubbabel and Jeshua, not Sheshbazzar, now lead the people. Tattenai, the pasha of Beyond-the-River province, questions the work. The reader's first impression may be that he is acting on the strength of the interdiction issued in ch. 4 after the agitation of the "people of the land." But the correspondence uncovers nothing of the stop-work order of Artaxerxes. Instead, a different version of the original permission of Cyrus vindicates the Judahites' project. Chapters 5–6 and ch. 4 are alternative versions of history.

Rhetorical Situation

Consequently, the rhetorical situation is different. The very first passage studied, Ezra 1:1-6, looked at the new conjunctions of power and authority in the post-Exilic world. Chapters 5–6 shift the intersection of past, present, and future in this restored order. The rhetoric situates the post-Exilic Judahite community within its history as viewed from the theological angle of the Temple.

Not only is the past still operative on the present; it is conformable to it. With the disappearance of Zerubbabel and the Davidic line there now emerges a new way to contemporize the past. The most striking rhetorical characteristic of this passage is the license with which the past is re-presented.

The passage fosters a sense of continuity with the past. The return of the Temple vessels, the reconstruction on the old site, the genealogies that link the people to previous generations, the construction like Solomon's (5:11: "we are building the house which was built many years ago which a great king of Israel built and finished")—all this suggests a striving for reassurance that they and their institutions stand in direct line with pre-Exilic Israel despite the loss of the Davidic dynasty. All political appearances notwithstanding, the past is not lost and the providence of YHWH is not withdrawn: "the eye of their God was upon the elders" (5:5).

It is a fundamental principle of modern biblical studies that the redaction of Scripture adjusts its retrospectives of history to meet certain theological goals. But here Ezra–Nehemiah boldly gives multiple versions of the past, back to back, in a way that solicits the conclusion that none needs to be reportorially accurate. Our attention is directed beyond the data to the question of history itself. History is not computable or even sequential here. It is prismatic. An event can be recounted in different forms that provide both continuity and plasticity. New realities are brought into focus by shifting the optic on the past. The past and the present shape one another in order to allow the repatriates to face the future better.

Rhetorical Strategies

LEADERSHIP

By the end of ch. 6 Zerubbabel has disappeared from the text despite the royal and messianic titles given him elsewhere by the prophets Haggai and Zechariah (Hag 2:20-23: "signet ring"; Zech 6:12: "the branch"). It may be that initially only a small group returned to Jerusalem with Sheshbazzar, the new Persian governor of Judah (Ezra 2:63). He is credited with laying the foundations for the new Temple and returning the sacred vessels taken by Nebuchadnezzar when he sacked the Temple in 587 (Ezra 4:14-15).

A few years later a second and larger group of exiles may have returned to Jerusalem under the leadership of Jehoiachin's grandson Zerubbabel and the priest Jeshua (Hag 1:1). Here the rhetorical strategy on the one hand is to avoid portraying Sheshbazzar's earlier expedition as abortive. Thus his return is alluded to in 5:16. On the other hand, it is important for the theology of the book that the group who continue the building under Zerubbabel and Jeshua be understood as the same who began it (Ezra 3:2, 8; 5:2). Thus neither Sheshbazzar nor Zerubbabel is mentioned by name at the end of the passage. We are told only that "the elders of the Jews built and prospered through the prophesying of Haggai the prophet and of Zechariah the son of Iddo" (6:14). This vagueness protects Sheshbazzar and also meets the rhetorical issue seen in the last chapter, the survival of Israel despite changing agents of authority.

INTRATEXTUAL REFERENCES

In bewildering fashion the passage overlays messages from various parties and times. After Haggai and Zechariah have inspired the repatriates, Tattenai and his associates ask the Judahites two questions: "Who gave you a decree to build this house and to complete (the preparation of) this material?" and "What are the names of the men who are building this building?" (5:3-4). We never know the Judahites' immediate response. Tattenai writes Darius a letter, and in it he quotes the written reply of the Judahite elders who give an idiosyncratic précis of Cyrus's decree.[1] Before we read the text of Tattenai's letter, however, we know that it has no effect on the Judahites, who continue their construction work. Tattenai asks for an archival search to determine if the work is unauthorized. We already know that it was forbidden in the previous chapter. Tattenai says he includes the names of the Judahites involved, but we do not see his list. Darius's answer quotes Cyrus's decree, but in a different version from that in ch. 1. As though Artaxerxes had never given judgment on the matter, Darius gives new warrant to the project and curses anyone who may want to stop it.

Chapters 5–6 remodel the past and turn the Judahites' defeat in ch. 4 into a victory. Omissions and alterations are blatant. Cyrus is quoted quite differently in ch. 6 than in ch. 1, and in Aramaic, not Hebrew.

---

[1] "Apomnemonysis" is the quotation of an approved authority.

Ezra 5:11 and 6:3, 7 are explicit that the project is a reconstruction of the Temple on the old site. Ezra 1:1-4 does not mention the place. There is another possible contradiction: Ezra 5:14 calls Sheshbazzar the "governor"; Ezra 1:8 names him the "prince." Missing here are references to the return from Exile, Cyrus's call from YHWH, and Sheshbazzar's background or ancestry. YHWH seems absent altogether here. The prophets are inspirational but wordless.

In 6:14 the elders of Israel "finish their building by command of the God of Israel and by the decree of Cyrus and Darius and Artaxerxes, king of Persia" (6:14). This is a concluding summary of the three movements of the history thus far,[2] but "decree" is in the singular as though there were only one. In fact there are three, two of which are contradictory. Artaxerxes in ch. 4 ordered the work stopped, not finished.

This free reshaping of the past is all the more striking in that in Ezra–Nehemiah the past is the criterion of the present. More precisely, written documents from the past are the foundation for actions in the present. Precedent and permission are the touchstones of authenticity. As discussed in the Introduction, the movement of events is generated through the succession of genealogies, lists, edicts, and letters. The text is actualized in the life of the community. Documents control the process of events. The divinely guided prophetic voices in Ezra 5:1 are quickly channelled into written documents that allow the action to occur. The pattern of documents invoking other documents and empowering action repeats itself periodically.[3]

Ezra 1–6 emphasizes the textuality of the book by its many self-references, internal allusions, and repetitions. "At the same time Tattenai came to them and said . . ." (5:3) is parallel to 4:2 where the enemies drew near to Zerubbabel and spoke. "They did not make them cease" (5:5) contrasts with 4:24: "Then they ceased the work and it ceased." Sacrifices according to the Law of Moses solemnize the rebuilding of the altar in 3:2 and the inauguration of the Temple in 6:17-18. Tattenai quotes himself word for word in his letter to the king: "Then we asked of those elders and spoke to them thus: 'Who gave you a decree to build this house and to complete (the preparation of) this material?'" (5:9; cf. 5:3). God is mentioned at the beginning and the end of the pas-

---

[2] See the Introduction for the description of the three movements of the history in Ezra 1–6. In 6:14 historical criticism notes that "Artaxerxes" could be Artaxerxes II (404–359). He ruled after Darius II (423–404), who might be the new king to whom Tattenai writes. In any case the ambiguity of the text stands.

[3] Tamara C. Eskenazi, *In an Age of Prose. A Literary Approach to Ezra–Nehemiah* (Atlanta, Ga.: Scholars, 1988) 59; eadem, "Ezra–Nehemiah: From Text to Actuality," in *Signs and Wonders: Biblical Texts in Literary Focus*, ed. J. Cheryl Exum. SBL.SS 18 (N.p.: Scholars, 1989) 166–67.

sage.[4] The king's decree says twice that the expenses are to be covered from his purse (6:4, 8). Finally, the priests and Levites purify themselves "as one," just as the people gathered "as one" for the reconstruction of the altar in 3:1.

PRESENT ESCHATOLOGY

Together with the divergent versions of the past, the effect of these echoes is to convey an assurance of both continuity and plasticity. The past is brought into the present by the many documents that legitimate the restoration of Judahite society. But the multiple redactions of those documents and the variations in the account of the people's history make the past a malleable thing, adaptable to a higher value than factuality.

The scholar Jon Levenson has argued that the rabbinical and Scriptural images of the "earthly Jerusalem" and the "heavenly Jerusalem" imply an essentially two-tiered world picture:

> The upper tier represents ultimate reality; it is the realm of God and his retinue. The lower tier is that of mundane reality, which is vulnerable to time, change, and flux, in short, open to history. . . . Zion represents the possibility of meaning above history, out of history, through an opening into the realm of the ideal. Mount Zion, the Temple on it, and the city around it are a symbol of transcendence, a symbol in Paul Tillich's sense of the word, something "which participates in that to which it points." . . . The ascent of the Temple mount is a movement toward a higher degree of reality, one from the world as manifestation to the world as essence, the world as the palpable handiwork of God and his dominion.[5]

The Temple is a microcosm of the world, "the world in nuce, and the world is the Temple in extenso."[6] Such an ideal universe is hinted at in the artfulness of the text. For all its confusing variations Ezra 1–6 is clearly the story of the reconstruction of the Temple. By the end of this section of Ezra–Nehemiah the restored Temple is once again the center of the community's life. But the perspective of the Temple already shapes this story of the reconstruction. Ezra–Nehemiah is written out

---

[4] Ezra 5:1; 6:12; 6:14. Repetition of a phrase at the beginning and end of a unit is technically called "epanalepsis."

[5] Jon D. Levenson, *Sinai and Zion. An Entry into the Jewish Bible.* New Voices in Biblical Studies 1, eds. Adela Yarbro Collins and John J. Collins (Minneapolis: Winston, 1985) 141–42, citing Paul Tillich, *Dynamics of Faith.* World Perspectives 10 (New York: Harper and Row, 1958) 42.

[6] Jon D. Levenson, "The Temple and the World," *JR* 64 (1984) 285.

of a proto-eschatology of the present in which the prophetic promises are fulfilled but YHWH's reign is not yet free.[7] By the end of Ezra–Nehemiah Israel will be rebuilt but still under foreign occupation: it is a "brief revival" only (Ezra 9:8). Ezra–Nehemiah never solves the theological contradiction of YHWH's sovereignty over Israel despite its Persian domination, but the rhetorical strategies of the book do already construct a narrative world in which history is transcended. The book has no easy answer to how the sacred and the secular combine in the post-Exilic world, but its repetitions, gaps, and compactions of events are a reflection of a theology in which raw, sequential time is already caught up in the eternity of the Temple. The failures of Israel's political history are not ignored, but they are made relative to a deeper sense of the meaning of history itself.

Therefore the rhetorical issue is more than continuity with the past. It is the broadening of perspective in order to see the locus of YHWH's intervention beyond the scale of the past and present. After Ezra restores the Israelites' worship in ch. 9 we will see in what way this marks the close of the history of Israel in the Hebrew Bible. According to the Hebrew Bible, God's intervention on Israel's behalf ends in its historical sequence with Ezra even though the life of Israel as a people continues. The witness of a continuing encounter with God in the period that follows will be made according to a different understanding and by means of other literary techniques.[8]

In the meantime here the restoration of the Temple is accomplished in an account that already anticipates the sense of time that the Temple effects and celebrates. It is fitting that ch. 6 ends with the liturgy of Passover and the institution of "the priests in their divisions and the Levites in their courses, for the service of God at Jerusalem, as it is written in the book of Moses" (6:18). Appropriately, the only reference in Ezra 5–6 that is above any rhetorical strategy is to this book of Moses. What portion it was of today's Hebrew Bible, if any, is disputed. Rhetorically, however, its status is clear. It is literally incomparable and unalterable because it is never quoted. It is the only document here that is without contradiction or adaptation. It is not open to archival verification or strategic rewording. It is set above even the decrees of the Persian ruler.

---

[7] Antonius H. J. Gunneweg, "Zur Interpretation der Bücher Esra–Nehemia: Zugleich ein Beitrag zur Methode der Exegese," *Congress Volume, Vienna, 1980* (Leiden: Brill, 1981) 161.

[8] Brevard S. Childs, *Biblical Theology of the Old and New Testaments. Theological Reflection on the Christian Bible* (Minneapolis: Fortress, 1993) 164–65.

Stylistic Devices

Several phrases suggest this eschatological sense of time whose nature is not defined by its sequence. We have mentioned how chs. 4 and
5 seem to follow in immediate succession. Also, the expression "at that
time" (Ezra 5:3) implies that the rebuilding started just as soon as Haggai and Zechariah preached. Verse 5:16 is a historian's conundrum:
"From then to now, it has been under construction, but it is not finished." What of the halt in construction against which Haggai and
Zechariah preached? At the start of the next episode (7:1) the phrase
"After these things" collapses a gap of about fifty years. These verses
make little positive sense; however, they fit into the kaleidoscope vision of a Temple-centered world.

Written documents are central to Ezra–Nehemiah, as we have mentioned. In chs. 5–6 many phrases from the letters follow the standard
pattern for such communication in the ancient Near East at that time.[9]
But the documents have been so deeply woven into the fabric of the
chapters that their distinction from each other or from the narration is
often unclear. In Tattenai's letter to Darius a smooth and complex transition shifts from the quoted reply of the Judahites to the end of Tattenai's own comments. (That is, vv. 5:15-17 move from Cyrus's remark to
Sheshbazzar cited in the Judahites' reply to Tattenai, which he quotes
in his letter to Darius before adding his own request to search for further documents!) In Darius's response the seam between Cyrus's
quoted decree and Darius's new instructions (6:5-6) is covered by the
use of the second person plural in each ("You shall deposit them . . . ."
"Now Tattenai, Shethar-bozenai and you their associates . . . keep
away from there!") Even when the transition is clearer the customary
formulaic introductions and conclusions of the letters are often trun-
cated, as in 4:22 and 6:3.[10] Narration, quotation, and instruction are in
a loosely-jointed convergence that reflects and intensifies the fusing of
past and present in the books.

The rhetorical creation of this vision sets Ezra–Nehemiah apart
from the apocalyptic preaching of the Books of Haggai and Zechariah.
Their "future passive eschatology" awaits God's intervention that
alone will bring a better future. In Ezra–Nehemiah the Judahites already construct in stone—and the book constructs in words—the first

[9] Refer especially to Victor (Avigdor) Hurowitz, *I Have Built You an Exalted
House: Temple Building in the Bible in Light of Mesopotamian and Northwest Semitic
Writing.* JSOT.S 115 (Sheffield: Sheffield Academic Press, 1992).

[10] Bezalel Porten, "The Address Formulae in Aramaic Letters: A New Collation
of Cowley 17," *RB* 90 (1983) 396–415.

elements of a Temple-world in which God's intervention will be given full play in an eschatological age. It is enough now that Darius's decree is irreversible. No one may disobey it and Darius prays that "the God who has caused his name to dwell there [may] overthrow any king or people" who harms the Temple (6:11).

Conclusion

"To see whether it really is so" (5:17): unintentionally, Tattenai's request to Darius becomes an equivocal comment on the rhetoric here. Written documents and the perlocutionary language of rulers[11] are normal instruments in the tiresome world of investigation, command, and political power. This is the everyday life in which, as an occupied people, the Judahites are fully immersed. But the rhetoric here has suborned these media into a rhetorical construction beyond any objectivity. In this perspective the fullest reality is the divine will. This inbreaking of "Temple truth" in a world still submitted to "political truth" is perhaps the rhetorical reason why the elders cried with both joy and sadness on seeing the reconstructed Temple foundations in 3:13. The size was to be six times that of Solomon's construction (6:3; cf. 1 Kings 6:2), but still the elders wept. All the dimensions are exactly described except the length. That is, the Temple is in existence but not yet, described but open-scaled, a delight but still to be anticipated. As the Temple is, so is the realm of history it celebrates and generates. It is ideal, but not in the sense that everything is systematic and transparent. The perfection to which it points is the holiness of YHWH alone, whose invisible presence supplies for the gaps in our understanding, and whose mysterious order is that of the eternal present.

---

[11] See the Introduction for more information on perlocutionary language. It is language that achieves something by its very utterance, like a legal will.

7:1   Now, after these things (or: words)
       in the reign (or: kingdom) of Artaxerxes,
       king of Persia,
       Ezra,
       son of Seraiah
       son of Azariah
       son of Hilkiah,
7:2   son of Shallum,
       son of Zadok,
       son of Ahitub,
7:3   son of Amariah,
       son of Azariah,
       son of Meraioth
7:4   son of Zerahiah,
       son of Uzzi,
       son of Bukki,
7:5   son of Abishu-a,
       son of Phinehas,
       son of Eleazar,
       son of Aaron, the first priest (or: chief priest)—
7:6   the same (lit. "he") Ezra went up from Babylon.
       He was a scribe skilled in the law of Moses
       which YHWH the God of Israel had given.
       And the king gave him—
       according to the hand of YHWH his God upon him—
       all he requested.
7:7   And some of the Israelites
       and some of the priests
       and Levites,
       and the singers
       and gatekeepers
       and the oblates
       went up to Jerusalem
       in the seventh year of Artaxerxes, the king.
7:8   And he came to Jerusalem
       in the fifth month,
       [which was] the seventh year of the king.
7:9   For on the first of the first month
       he fixed the ascent from Babylon
       and on the first of the fifth month

	he came to Jerusalem,
	according to the good hand of his God upon him.
7:10	For Ezra had set his heart to inquire [after] the law of Yʜᴡʜ
	and to act upon (lit. "do")
	and to teach in Israel law
	and ordinance.
7:11	This is the copy of the letter
	which the King Artaxerxes gave to Ezra,
	the priest,
	the scribe,
	the scribe of matters of the commandments of Yʜᴡʜ and his laws [laid] upon Israel.
7:12	"Artaxerxes,
	king of kings,
	to Ezra,
	the priest,
	the scribe of the law of the God of heaven,
	plenitude (lit. "all," i.e., "peace"?)!
	and now:
7:13	From me a decree
	that any one in my kingdom from the people of Israel,
	its priests,
	and the Levites
	volunteering to go to Jerusalem with you
	may go.
7:14	For [you are] sent from before the king and his seven counsellors
	to inquire about Judah and Jerusalem
	on [the basis of] the law of your God
	which is in your hand
7:15	and to transport some silver and gold
	which the king and his counsellors volunteered [to give] to the God of Israel
	whose dwelling is in Jerusalem,
7:16	together with any silver or gold
	which you will find anywhere in the province of Babylon,
	as well as the volunteer offerings of the people and the priests
	which they volunteeer for the house of their God
	which is in Jerusalem.
7:17	Consequently with this money diligently buy bulls,
	rams,
	lambs,
	and the fitting (lit. "their") meal offerings

and drink offerings,

and you are to offer them on the altar of the house of your
God in Jerusalem.

7:18   And what is good to you and your brothers to do with the
rest of the silver and gold

according to the will of your God,

you may do [it].

7:19   And the vessels

which were given to you for the service (or: cult) of the house
of your God

you shall render in full before the God of Jerusalem.

7:20   The rest of what is needed for the house of your God

which it falls to you to give,

you may give it from the treasuries of the king (lit. the house
of the king's treasures).

7:21   And herewith I,

King Artaxerxes,

issue a decree to all the treasurers of Beyond the River:

that whatever Ezra,

the priest,

the scribe of the Law of the God of heaven

shall ask you

shall be done diligently,

7:22   up to a maximum of a hundred talents of silver,

a hundred kors of wheat,

a hundred baths of wine,

a hundred baths of oil,

and salt without limit (lit. "written," i.e., "requirement").

7:23   Whatever is of the decree of the God of heaven

is to be done exactly for the house of the God of heaven,

lest there be (or: why should there be?) [divine] wrath (lit.
"foam") on the kingdom of the king and his sons.

7:24   Be it known to you (lit. "they inform you")

that on all the priests,

the Levites,

the cantors,

the porters,

the oblates,

the servants (or: cultic servants) of this house of God,

it is not permitted to impose

tribute,

tax,

or dues.

7:25   And you,
Ezra,
according to the wisdom of your God
which is in your hand,
appoint arbitrators
and judges
who will be judges of all the people in Beyond the River
      [Province];
all those who know the laws of your God,
and any who do not know them,
you (lit. "you" plural) must instruct (lit. "make them know").

7:26   But anyone who does not do the law of your God
and the law of the king,
judgment is to be diligently done against him,
either death,
or banishment,
or confiscation (or: fine? lit. "punishment of goods"),
or imprisonment."

7:27   "Blessed [be] YHWH the God of our fathers
who has put (lit. "given") thus (lit. "like this") in the heart
      of the king
to beautify the house of YHWH
which is in Jerusalem,

7:28   and who has extended lovingkindness to me
before the king
and his counsellors
and all the officials of the king,
the heroes.
So, I took courage
according to the hand of YHWH my God upon me,
and I gathered from Israel leading [men]
to go up with me."

Chapter Four
EZRA 7

Introduction

This chapter seems to follow immediately in time: "Now, after these things (or: words)." Whether the events or the speech in the preceding pericope are meant is unclear in the Hebrew. In any case the difference is slight because in chs. 5–6 rhetoric has reshaped history. That is, words have taken control of events in the text.

Rhetorical Situation

We saw in the last chapter that the rhetoric compensated for the loss of Zerubbabel and the Davidic line. The speeches and letters set a bearing on the past through a vision of the world in which history is recouped by an act of interpretation. The Judahites under Persian occupation are not the masters of their present time but the rhetoric of Ezra–Nehemiah is an instrument to claim their past. The redimensioned structure of history in chs. 5–6 is a function of the conviction that the divine will is the only true measure of reality.

Since YHWH is not directly active in the story that insight elicits another question. How does one know YHWH's will and so interpret the meaning of experience? Now a new leader is presented whose will is united to YHWH's. The nature of his competence and authority holds together diverse elements in the Judahites' life of faith. Having established in ch. 1 that the community still exists because it is still willed by YHWH, the text now introduces Ezra, who will teach them how to respond to this providence. How should they root themselves in face of the relativity of historical understanding demonstrated in chs. 5–6? How shall they make their home in the eddying flow of time? And how should their experience of solitude due to defeat be balanced with the conviction of grace from their renewed festival worship (6:22)?

41

The redactional problem in ch. 7 is how to integrate texts on Temple worship with appeals to the Law. Historical-critical studies unravel strands of at least two traditions and discuss the relation between the priestly and scribal crafts in view of the Exile. On one level these issues are resolved in the description and utterances of Ezra. His rhetorical presence is itself the harmony of prophecy, Law, and worship. His triple sanctions from YHWH, the narrator, and the king prepare his mission, which is to proclaim the possibility of inserting the real into the categories of the sacred.

Rhetorical Strategies

Most of chs. 5 and 6 was taken up with the correspondence between Tattenai and Darius. The prophets Haggai and Zechariah were influential but silent. The Judahites were quoted only in the letter of their enemies. At the end of ch. 6 we had a brief insight into their state of mind and the king's: "they celebrated the dedication of this house of God with joy. . . . And they kept the feast of unleavened bread seven days with joy; for YHWH had made them joyful, and had turned the heart of the king of Assyria to them" (6:18, 22).

Ezra is now introduced, and he too is wordless at first. As for the rhetorical audience, this silence means that the addressees are not yet the Judahites themselves. We listeners to the text share privileged access to the letter that the king writes to Ezra (7:12-26). We hear about his high character and pedigree in the narrator's apostrophe in 7:1-10. Both the narrator and the king give him a grand double title: priest and scribe (vv. 11, 12).

The pericope has epideictic qualities, that is, it presents the praises of some person. It is one of the principles of Old Testament characterization that the biblical narrator is taciturn but trustworthy. When the narrator tells us that Ezra was "skilled in the law of Moses" and that "the king gave him—according to the hand of YHWH his God upon him—all he requested (v. 6)" we may believe him freely. These epithets, rare in Scripture, are a judgment and they invite us to judgment, too. This privileged insight into the "heart" of Ezra removes any doubts about his worth, but it leaves open the question of how the Judahites will be convinced of what we have been told authoritatively.

As mentioned in the Introduction, one of the three modes of argumentation is called "ethical," that is, it is based on the "ethos" of the orator. Ethos is the character one demonstrates to a particular audience in order to inspire its confidence. One must at least show oneself to be reasonable, sincere, and sympathetic. "Ethical proofs" usually apply to the speaker. But Ezra is silent until v. 27 and then it is unclear whether he delivers his prayer (vv. 27-28) aloud to others or to himself. As a result we believe his described qualities all the more because he himself has not yet promoted them. In contrast, in ch. 4 the "people of the land" made an ethical argument that never won us over and was reversed politically in ch. 5.

The pericope is also an argument from the highest level of authority: the narrator, the king, and YHWH himself all favor Ezra.[1] Rhetorical theorists say that such arguments of authority are based on the "structure of reality." They work experientially, not logically. Here the argumentation fits the reality of Ezra–Nehemiah's world in which the narrator is reliable, the king politically powerful, and YHWH divinely sovereign. Since we accept the narrator, the king, and YHWH we also accept their endorsement of Ezra. We are not encouraged, for example, to question that his authority expands even within the course of the chapter, from "Judah and Jerusalem" to "all the people in Beyond the River [Province]" (vv. 14, 25).

Such an argument of authority is appropriate here because Ezra's task in the coming chapters will be to bring the Judahites to see the full truth of their own experience. The re-presentation of history according to the eternal synchroneity of the Temple (chs. 5–6) is followed now by the presentation of Ezra according to the eternal standards of Torah. His mission will point to the deep structure of reality defined by the Law, and he will urge the Judahites to shape their lives according to these norms, to raise the profane to the level of the sacred. "For Ezra had set his heart to enquire [after] the law of YHWH and to act upon (lit. "do") and to teach in Israel law and ordinance" (7:10).

As well as "ethos" or character, an appeal is made in ch. 7 through arguments based loosely on reasoning or "logos." In a kind of argumentation called "double hierarchy" Ezra wins our approval because we associate his values with those of YHWH and the narrator that we already accept.

The premises the audience is expected to share are that the king is powerful and the Torah is good. Built on that is the following enthymeme. As always with enthymemes, the first member (in parentheses) is the unstated or presumed proposition:

- (The Law expresses the will of YHWH.)
- Ezra is an expert in the Law (v. 6).
- Therefore Ezra is an expert in the will of YHWH.

---

[1] *"Argumentum ad verecundiam"* is the technical term for an appeal to the reverence of authority.

Upon this is constructed a second enthymeme, a polysyllogism that incorporates the conclusion of the first:

- (The king is powerful and can give anything.)
- The king gives Ezra everything according to YHWH's hand on him (v. 6).
- [From the first enthymeme:] Ezra is an expert in the will of YHWH.
- Therefore the king gives Ezra anything at all.

After these arguments by authority and quasi-logic Ezra will be established in our minds as a reliable figure. Future arguments can thus be "of the person," based on the link between the person and his acts. Reactions to his actions then run along the lines that "we know him; such and such is true to his character."[2]

The long epithetical introduction of Ezra is accompanied by his genealogy. Ezra–Nehemiah is generally short of any lengthy titles. On the other hand this is the longest personal pedigree in Scripture. It contrasts sharply with the blunt title "Artaxerxes, King of Persia." Like the version of history in chs. 5–6, this account of Ezra's past is theologically constructed. He is not called "son" of his father but of Seraiah, the last chief priest before the Exile. That is to say, Ezra is his legitimate descendent in a link spanning time and family. This list begins with Ezra and works back to Aaron. As a "scribe skilled in the law of Moses," Ezra is the successor to Moses. As a priest he is a successor to Aaron. This double reference to Moses the Law-giver and to Aaron the priest enhances Ezra's prestige. It is the first and only place in Scripture where the offices are explicitly combined or fused.[3] It is also another way in which ch. 7 creates the correlation of various traditions in the language around and about Ezra. The details of the passage, discussed below, work out this correlation from a rhetorical equivalency between YHWH's Law and Persia's, YHWH's will and Ezra's. In the last chapter it was affirmed that the fullest reality is YHWH's will. Now his will is to be interpreted in prophetic language through the Law for a restored community that preserves, celebrates, and transforms its historical memory in the cult.

[2] Olivier Reboul, *Introduction à la rhétorique: théorie et pratique* (2nd ed., Collection 1er cycle, Paris: Presses universitaires de France, 1994) 181.

[3] Tamara C. Eskenazi, *In an Age of Prose. A Literary Approach to Ezra–Nehemiah* (Atlanta, Ga.: Scholars, 1988) 75.

Stylistic Devices

Ezra enters the story without a birth narrative like Moses' or Samson's and without a narrative of YHWH's call to him like that of Jeremiah or Isaiah. In the first sentence, between the subject (v. 1: "Ezra") and the verb (v. 6: "went up") his long genealogy begins to tie together his person, Israel's past, and his current action of traveling to Jerusalem. The broken syntax is technically called "anacoluthon": "Ezra, son of . . . the same (lit. "he") Ezra went up . . . ." It creates an expectancy around Ezra that is fulfilled when he is praised as a "scribe skilled in the law of Moses" to whom the king gives all that he requests.

When the king himself repeats that Ezra is a scribe versed in the commandments (v. 11) the commonality of values among the king, YHWH, the narrator, and Ezra is promoted. The king's mandate for an inquiry on the basis of the law of [Ezra's] God continues the association (vv. 13-14). It climaxes here in v. 23 where the king decrees whatever the God of heaven commands, and in v. 26 with the practical equivalence of "the law of [Ezra's] God and the law of the king." One recalls the same in 6:14: "They finished their building by command of the God of Israel and by the decree of Cyrus and Darius and Artaxerxes, king of Persia." But now the focusing figure is Ezra.

In 1:1 "the spirit of YHWH" worked on Cyrus. Now Ezra has the same effect on Cyrus's successor, and the seam between the royal decree and Ezra's own words is made fine to the point of confusion (vv. 26-27). Ezra's prayer has no introductory narrative and it is immediately glued to the decree by a particle whose antedecent is the decree itself: ". . . YHWH . . . has put (lit. "given") *thus* (lit. "like this") in the heart of the king."

In 1:1-24 the people of the land gingerly brought the king around to a change in his policy without belittling him. It was a political ploy. Here the king effectively places himself below Ezra, and for theological reasons. Schematically in quasi-logic:

- (Ezra mediates the Law of YHWH.)
- To avoid YHWH's anger the king wants YHWH's Law obeyed (v. 23).
- Therefore the king obeys Ezra.

Ezra is the more admirable because his actions and beliefs are coherent. Self-consistency is an important element in arguments based on the structure of reality and on the person. The similarity of some words makes the point here. He "had set his heart to *inquire* [after] the *law* of YHWH" (v. 10) and he is sent "to *inquire* about Judah and Jerusalem on [the basis of] the *law* of [his] God which is in [his] hand." (The two Hebrew verbs for "inquire" are close in meaning.) The *"hand* of YHWH" is upon him, and the Law is *"in his hand"* (vv. 7, 14).

He will *"act upon* (lit. "do") and *teach* in Israel law and ordinance" (v. 10). Ezra is so much the master of himself and of the Law that he is the only one in the Old Testament to whom the words "doing" and "teaching/learning" are applied in that order.[4] He teaches just what he himself practices. (In every other reference to the commandments the order of these verbs is reversed.) The unusual order of "doing and teaching" here recalls Exod 24:7 where after Moses has read the book of the covenant the people proclaim: "All that YHWH has spoken we will *do,* and we will be *obedient* (lit. "will hear")." Ezra himself will soon read the Law to the renewed community.

His first words are unique in Scripture: "Blessed [be] YHWH, the God of our fathers" (v. 27). Significantly, Deut 26:7-8 comes closest: literally "Then we cried to YHWH *the God of our fathers,* and YHWH heard our voice, and saw our affliction, our toil, and our oppression; and YHWH brought us out of Egypt with a mighty hand . . . ." In the whole Hebrew Bible, to Ezra alone are applied the following Hebrew phrases: he "inquires [after] the law," he takes "courage according to the hand of YHWH" (v. 28 and 9:9), "YHWH has extended lovingkindness" to him (v. 28 and 9:9). Only he and Solomon enjoy "the wisdom of God" (7:25, 1 Kings 3:28). "The good hand of God" is on him alone, the people under him and Nehemiah (7:9; 8:18; Neh 2:8).

EZRA AND THE PAST

Ezra's originality does not mean he is isolated from the biblical context. Chapter 7 inserts him into Israel's past, present, and future. His first line of contact with the past is his genealogy. Another is his fixed date of departure from Babylon in the first month and before Passover, like the Exodus from Egypt in the **P** tradition (Exod 12:2; Num 33:3). His first words (v. 27) evoke the ancient "fathers" of Israel in a declarative psalm of praise that is a common biblical genre. What rhetoric calls a "principle of communion" is thus created with the Judahites through their heritage.

EZRA AND THE PRESENT

Set in the present moment are his concrete task and his qualifications. The mission is described mundanely in the matter-of-fact lists of people, goods, and quantities. Ezra is a man of action: he "comes up" (v. 6, repeated in v. 28). He is not a finely sketched character like David

----

[4] "To learn" and "to teach" are the same root in Hebrew.

or Jeremiah with the inner substance of self-reflection and development. Instead, he has presence in the text by virtue of our clarity of insight into his giant talents and energy.

The rhetoric builds on these prosaic details to make of Ezra a bond between the king and YHWH. He is sent from "before" the king and will render the treasure "before" the God of Jerusalem (vv. 14, 19: the same Aramaic word). Ezra has set his "heart" to study the Law of YHWH who put it in the "heart" of the king to beautify the Temple (vv. 10, 27; also 6:22: the same Hebrew word). In the Bible the heart signifies the whole of one's being. Ezra is not a "realistic" character in any literary sense, but neither is he superspiritualized or thrust beyond the political realm.

EZRA AND THE FUTURE

He is linked to the future of Israel more subtly. As the chapter ends he is ready to take action, with the leading men of Israel around him, and the description of his mission employs words whose connotation arches toward the future. For example, a number of words in Ezra 7 direct the careful listener to Isaiah 60 and its vision of the rebuilding of the Temple. The king says he is mandating Ezra lest the wrath (lit. "foam") of YHWH beset him (v. 23), and Ezra thanks YHWH that he has moved the king's heart to beautify the Temple (v. 27). Only here is the Hebrew or Aramaic word for "wrath" used by a foreigner to connote divine anger. Elsewhere it occurs with the rare word "beautify, glorify" only in Isaiah 60, whose other words and themes re-echo all through Ezra 7:

> Your heart shall thrill and rejoice. . . . I will *glorify* my glorious house. . . . For the coastlands shall wait for me, the ships of Tarshish first, to bring your children from far away, their silver and gold with them, for the name of the LORD your God, and for the Holy One of Israel, because he has *glorified* you. . . . Foreigners shall build up your walls, and their kings shall minister to you; for in my *wrath* I struck you down, but in my favor I have had mercy on you. . . . For the nation and kingdom that will not serve you shall perish; those nations shall be utterly laid waste . . . that I might be *glorified*. . . . I am the LORD; in its time I will accomplish it quickly (Isa 60:5-22).

"Skilled" (v. 6) is used four times in Scripture of someone who stands before kings or YHWH or, in Isa 16:5, of a figure who is himself enthroned.[5]

The two "hand" images are telling. "According to the hand of YHWH on . . ." is peculiar to Ezra, of whom it is used twice (vv. 6, 9). Apart from him the "hand of YHWH" is "with" or "upon" someone only

---

[5] Isa 16:5; Ps 45:1; Prov 22:29; Ezra 7:9.

in prophetic passages.[6] The Law is "in [someone's] hand" exclusively in the case of Ezra here (v. 14), of Moses, and of the prophets.[7] "Wrath," "heart," and "law in [someone's] hand" are clustered elsewhere only in Zech 7:12 where the Return from Exile is hoped for. But in Zechariah the people do not listen to the Law. Will they heed Ezra now?

> They made their *hearts* adamant in order not to hear the *law* and the words that the LORD of hosts had sent by his spirit through (lit. *"in the hand of"*) the former prophets. Therefore great *wrath* came from the LORD of hosts (Zech 7:12).

Ezra's return of the Temple vessels is also a prophetic motif, echoing Isa 52:11-12:[8]

> Depart, depart, go out from there! touch no unclean thing; go out from the midst of it, purifying yourselves, you who bear the vessels of the LORD. For you shall not go out in haste, and you shall not go in flight, for the LORD will go before you, and the God of Israel will be your rear guard.

Conclusion

What Ezra lacks in fullness of narrative character is made up for in antecedence, prestige, and expectation. His uniqueness notwithstanding, he is placed within the canonical envelope by the use of legal, prophetic, and cultic language.[9] He is literally "canonized" by the rhetoric of ch. 7. Like an echo chamber his own words and those concerning him blend the language of tendencies that were not always in harmony in the Judahite religion of the day: Law, prophecy, and cult. Here not the actions but the language of these institutions has been attached to him. He is a priest, but here he does not perform sacrifices like one. The introduction to him and his mission uses prophetic language but he is not a prophet in his role or manner. He is a master of the Law, second only to Moses in rabbinic tradition,[10] but he shares nothing of

[6] Elijah, Elisha, YHWH's servants in Third Isaiah, and very commonly Ezekiel in, respectively, 1 Kings 18:46; 2 Kings 3:15; Isa 66:14; Ezekiel *passim*. Ezekiel is a figure who also combines the priestly and prophetic traditions.

[7] Dan 9:10; Neh 8:14; 9:14; 10:29; 2 Chron 33:8; 34:14, where the same expression in places means "by means of."

[8] H. G. N. Williamson, *Ezra and Nehemiah* (Sheffield: JSOT Press, 1987) 85.

[9] On the inchoate eschatological tone of Ezra–Nehemiah see Antonius H. J. Gunneweg, "Zur Interpretation der Bücher Esra–Nehemia: Zugleich ein Beitrag zur Methode der Exegese," *Congress Volume, Vienna, 1980* (Leiden: Brill, 1981) 160–61; Otto Plöger, *Theokratie und Eschatologie*, WMANT (Neukirchen: Neukirchener Verlag, 1959) 131–35.

[10] Brevard S. Childs, *Biblical Theology of the Old and New Testaments. Theological Reflection on the Christian Bible* (Minneapolis: Fortress, 1993) 164; David L. Petersen,

Moses' call, theophanies, or heroic style of leadership. The description of the Temple's reconstruction in chs. 5–6 interpreted the sense of history beyond its sequential pattern. The description of Ezra and his mission uses biblical language beyond the categories of traditional genres.

Scholarship on Ezra–Nehemiah has often examined the interplay of the legal and cultic traditions. The influence of each at the time of the book's composition is a matter of much discussion. So is the fate of the prophetic movement after the Exile. Here the chapter smoothly syncretizes their vocabulary and mandates the restoration of the Temple sacrifices according to the Law by Ezra, whose mission is described in prophetic language. The two royal orders here are both cultic and juridical in scope: to bring up the Temple treasure and to inquire about Judah and Jerusalem according to the Law of YHWH. We will see how Ezra's own actions and words become more cultic in Ezra 9–10.

Ezra's deeper purpose is to conform the society to sacred principles. We saw in chs. 4–5 how the account of history was re-visioned through the perspective of the eternal divine will. This perspective is now brought into the present and embodied in the rhetorical person of Ezra. In his words and description transitory worldly values are radically adjusted. Just as the foreign king Cyrus was YHWH's agent in ch. 1, so now King Artaxerxes will do whatever Ezra wants. Ezra will appoint judges to enact the law of Persia "according to the wisdom of [his] God" in a world in which the god's law embraces the king's (vv. 25-26). The Law informs and also responds to experience.

There is no interest here in "faith and reason" or "church and state." Israel is called to a dialectical world that embraces the utilitarian and the covenantal. Israel's post-Exilic tragedy—and each society's, always—is to be unable to root itself in either the provisional or the perpetual. The bridge for Israel is the Law, and its messenger here is a man whose singular rhetorical presence anticipates the harmony that can only come fully in the future.

Ezra is not an "eschatological figure" any more than he is a prophet, but the language used of him proclaims that any redemption of the world is coming not in a higher sphere but via the world itself, through the adaptation of empirical reality to the ideal patterns of the Law. Ezra's words show him ready to build a community of Law and worship that contains both the past, which it refashions and revivifies, and the future that is always to come, but within the life of the community preserved by its cultic memory.

---

ed., *The Temple in Persian Period Prophetic Texts*. Second Temple Studies: I. Persian Period. (Sheffield: JSOT Press, 1991) 159. See *b.Sanh.* 21b-22, *b.Torah* 20a-20b.

9:1   And when these [events] were finished
       the chiefs approached me
       saying,
       "The people of Israel,
       the priests,
       and the Levites
       have not separated themselves
       from the peoples of the lands
       according to their abominations
       —from the Canaanites,
       Hittites,
       Perizzites,
       Jebusites,
       Ammonites,
       Moabites,
       Egyptians
       and Amorites—

9:2   For (*kî*) they have taken some of their daughters [as wives]
       for themselves and their sons
       so that the holy seed has become intermingled (lit. "plural")
           with the peoples of the lands
       And the hand of the chiefs and the officials was first in this
           unfaithfulness."

9:3   And when I heard this thing
       I tore my garment and my cloak
       and I pulled out some of the hair of my head and my beard.
       And I remained seated dumbfounded.
       To me gathered all who trembled at the words of the God of
           Israel
       on account of the unfaithfulness of the Exile.

9:4   And I sat dumbfounded until the evening sacrifice.

9:5   And at the evening sacrifice I rose from my humiliation
       with my garment and my cloak torn
       and bowed down on my knees
       and spread my palms to YHWH my God

9:6   and I said
       "My God,
       I am ashamed
       and mortified
       to raise,

my God,
my face to you.
for our iniquities have increased to over [our] head[s]
and our guilt has grown to the skies.

9:7 From the days of our fathers we [have been] in great guilt
until this day.
And because of our iniquities, we,
our kings,
[and] our priests
have been given into the hand of kings of the lands,
to the sword,
to captivity,
to pillage,
and to open shame (lit. "shame of face"), as this day.

9:8 But now for a brief moment
there has been favor from YHWH our God
to leave us an escaped remnant
and to give us a secure hold (lit. "peg") in the place of his
holiness
[so that] our God may cheer us (lit. "brighten our eyes")
and give us brief (or: a measure of) revival in our slavery.

9:9 For (kî) we are slaves;
but in our slavery our God did not abandon us
but has extended to us lovingkindness in the face of the
kings of Persia
to give us revival,
to erect the house of our God
and to restore (lit. "set up") its ruins
and to give us a fence in Judah and in Jerusalem.

9:10 And now
what shall we say,
our God,
after this?
for (kî) we have abandoned your commandments

9:11 which you commanded through (lit. "in the hand of") your
slaves the prophets,
saying,
'The land
which you are going in to possess (lit. "it"),
(lit. "it") [is] an impure land
in the impurity of the peoples of the lands,
in their abominations
whereby they have filled it with (lit. "in") their uncleanness

9:12   from end to end (lit. "from mouth to mouth").
        And now
        your daughters—do not give [them] to their sons
        and their daughters—do not take [them] for your sons.
        And do not inquire after their welfare and good ever, so that
        you may strengthen
        and eat the good of the land
        and make it an inheritance to your sons forever.'
9:13   After all that came upon us
        because of [lit. "in"] our deeds of evil and our great guilt
        although *(kî)* you,
        our God,
        have punished [us] less than (lit. "below") our iniquities
            [merit]
        and have given us an escaped remnant like this.
9:14   Shall we again break your commandments
        and marry into the peoples of these abominations?
        Shall you not be angry with us
        to [the point of] destroying
        until there is no survivor or escaped remnant?
9:15   YHWH, God of Israel,
        righteous [are] you!
        Yet (or: for, *kî)* we are left an escaped remnant as this day.
        Behold us before you in our guilt,
        although *(kî)* there is no standing before you in this matter
            (or: in such a condition, lit. "on this")."

10:1   Now as Ezra was praying
        and confessing,
        weeping and prostrate before the house of God,
        a very large crowd from Israel assembled around
            (lit. "to") him,
        men and women and children,
        indeed *(kî)* the people wept abundantly (lit. "much
            weeping").
10:2   And Shecaniah, the son of Jehiel from the family of (lit.
            "sons of") Elam, replied to Ezra,
        saying
        "We have betrayed our God
        and married (lit. "made to dwell") foreign women from the
            peoples of the land,
        but now there is hope for Israel concerning this.
10:3   And now let us make a covenant to (with? before?) our God

to send away (lit. "make go out") all the women

and the one[s] born from them according to the counsel of
my lord (or: my Lord)

and those who tremble at the commandments of our God.

And, according to the Law, let it be done!

10:4 Arise! for *(kî)* on you [rests] the matter.

And (or: but) we [will be] with you.

Be strong and act (lit. "do")!"

10:5 So Ezra arose

and made the chiefs of the priests,

the Levites,

and all Israel take an oath to act (lit. "do") according to this
word.

And they took an oath.

10:6 And Ezra arose from before the house of God

and went to the room of Jehohanan the son of Eliashib.

He went there (or: spent the night?),

without eating bread

or drinking water

for *(kî)* he was mourning over the unfaithfulness of the exiles
(lit. "Exile").

10:7 They made the word (lit. "voice") pass in Judah and Jerusalem to all the sons of the Exile to gather [in] Jerusalem.

10:8 "Anyone who does not come in three days

according to the advice of the chiefs and the elders

will cause to be confiscated all his belongings

and he will be separated from the congregation of the Exile."

10:9 So all the men of Judah and Benjamin gathered [in] Jerusalem
within three days

—it was the ninth month on the twentieth of the month—

and all the people sat in the square of the house of God.

They were shaking on [account of] the matter and the rains.

10:10 Ezra the priest arose

and said to them,

"You are unfaithful

when you married (lit. "made to dwell") foreign women

[thereby] adding to the guilt of Israel."

10:11 But now, give thanks to YHWH the God of your fathers,

and do his will

and separate yourselves

from the peoples of the land and from the foreign women."

10:12 And the whole crowd answered

and said [in] a great voice,

"Indeed! *(kēn)*
According to your word, [it is] upon us to do!

10:13   But the people are many,
and [it is] the time of the rains,
and there is no strength to stand in the open,
and the work is not for one day or two
for *(kî)* many of us transgressed in this matter.

10:14   Let our chiefs stand [in] for the whole crowd.
[Let] all who are in our towns
who have married (lit. "made to dwell") foreign women
come at appointed times
and with them the town elders of every town
and their judges
so that (or: until) we may avert our God's anger from us."

10:15   Only (or: but) Jonathan the son of Asahel
and Jahzeiah the son of Tikvah stood against this,
but Meshullam
and Shabbethai the Levite helped them.

10:16   And the sons of the Exile did thus *(kēn)*.
Ezra the priest chose (lit. "were separated") men [as] heads
        of families (lit. "fathers")
[according] to the house of their fathers
and all of them [were registered] by name.
And they sat on the first day (lit. "one day") in the tenth
        month to investigate the matter.

10:17   And they concluded [dealing] with all the men who had
married (lit. "made to dwell") foreign women on the first
day (lit. "one day") of the first month.

Chapter Five
EZRA 9–10

Introduction

CHAPTER EIGHT

The events and descriptions of ch. 8 develop the arguments of ch. 7. A names list opens the chapter, which is then stitched to ch. 7 by the resumptive repetition of "to gather": Ezra "gathered from Israel leading [men]" (7:28) and he again gathers the people by the river for the departure (8:15). Between these verses the list is a shortened variation of the one in ch. 2; the lineage is no longer Zadokite but Aaronite, the family from which Ezra is descended. It enumerates the community and its leaders with whom Ezra will work for the transformation of Israel. Like the portrait of Ezra in ch. 7 this list is composed to bear a particular image of the people. It is in three parts, first the priestly families, secondly—but only secondly!—the descendant of the royal line of David (Hattush, cf. 1 Chron 3:22) and last, twelve families of the laity. Only twelve families are mentioned, perhaps to reflect the twelve tribes of Israel. (In 8:35 they will offer twelve bulls.) The number of a dozen could also be meant simply as a round number: multiples of ten are used throughout for the numbers of the families. The list is an ordered profile of Ezra's companions as the sole legitimate representatives and heirs of Israel.

Chapter 8 runs along the lines of chs. 5 to 7 concerning the cult's effect on the world and society. This theology makes understandable the ascendancy of the priestly families here, as well as the care given to the consignment of the Temple treasure by Ezra and his redoubled effort to bring along Levites although some were already in Jerusalem. The arrival in Jerusalem was on the first day of Ab, the fifth month, in which the destruction of the First Temple was commemorated, but Ezra delayed entering the city until the twelfth, the day of the month on which Passover is celebrated.[1] In v. 24 responsibility for the treasure is vested in twelve priests, according to the instructions in Numbers

---

[1] Ezra 7:8; 8:22, 31; cf. 2 Kings 25:8; Zech 7:3; 8:19; Exod 12:11; Num 33:3.

3–4 about the custody and movement of tabernacle furnishings. They are "separated" for the task, using a Hebrew word that is almost exclusively applied to the cult and purity. They and the objects in their charge are then "holy" (v. 28) in the sense of "set apart," again a word from the cultic vocabulary. The fast, too, is a gesture of worship,[2] and the unit closes with a sacrifice in 10:19. Although there is no action in the precincts of the Temple proper in ch. 8, its actions and descriptions broaden the inclusion of worship in the society to be reconstructed.

Chapter 8 also makes some allusions to the prophetic traditions and language, as Ezra 1 and 7 did. The successful journey is called "straight," perhaps recalling the Exilic Isaiah's call to make straight the way for the homecoming exiles (Isa 40:3). The only other occurrences of the Hebrew phrase for "straight way" are 1 Sam 12:23, where the prophet Samuel prays for a straight and good way for his people, and Ps 107:7, a commemoration of the Exodus: "he led them by a straight way, till they reached a city to dwell in."

As elsewhere in Ezra–Nehemiah ch. 8 elicits the motif of the Exodus and applies it as the Exilic prophets did to the return from Babylon. Despite the enormous value of the treasure[3] Ezra refuses an escort: the desert has always been a place to test one's sole faith in YHWH. Since the repatriation from Babylon is in several waves the Exodus, as evoked here, is open to various generations with no opprobrium attached to those who leave only now. In this way, as in the portrayal of history in chs. 5-6, the past is accessible for theological reinterpretation in every generation.

Ezra's preparation for the Return and entry into Jerusalem is both pragmatic and devout. He sees to the material and cultic details in a way coherent with his introduction in ch. 7 as one who applies the divine and civic laws with justice.

COMMUNITY-BUILDING AND EXOGAMY

Ezra no sooner arrives than an issue is brought before him for judgment. As in ch. 7, time moves swiftly: "And when these [events] were

---

[2] Joseph Blenkinsopp, *Ezra–Nehemiah* (Philadelphia: Westminster, 1988) 168, describes how, in the pre-exilic period, fasting was practiced as an accompaniment to mourning or in a situation of national or individual emergency (Judg 20:26; Jer 14:12; 36:6, 9; Pss 35:13; 69:11 [10]; 109:24). It became more common later, after the fall of the southern kingdom (Zech 7:2-7; 8:19; cf. Isa 58:3-9). As here, it often acted as reinforcement of prayer: Neh 9:1; Dan 9:3; 2 Chron 20:3.

[3] The treasure as described amounts to the annual salary of between 100,000 and 500,000 men according to David J. A. Clines, *Ezra, Nehemiah, Esther* (Grand Rapids: Eerdmans, 1984) 113!

finished . . . ." The chiefs approach him and say that the people have intermarried.

In Ezra–Nehemiah as we read it now a long period of post-Exilic confusion draws to an end when the repatriates succeed in organizing to rebuild the Temple. They dedicate "this house of God with joy" (7:16), and they keep the Passover. Only then does Ezra, the namesake of the book, appear. He now starts the second phase of the revival of Israel: he seeks to reconstitute the community itself.

His rebuilding of Israelite society is the counterpart of the restoration of the city walls by Nehemiah. Ezra wants to build a metaphorical "fence in Judah and in Jerusalem" (9:9). Both projects involve circumscription—of the people ethnically and of the city physically. Ezra tells the people that they are to renew themselves by repenting and putting aside their foreign wives and children.

The earlier chapters have already distinguished between inside and outside groups. In 1:5 the faithful who went up to build the Temple were "all [those] whose spirit God had roused," who were ready to embrace change. Then the families without genealogies were removed from the priesthood (2:62). In ch. 4 the "people of the land" were kept from the project to rebuild the Temple. At the end of ch. 6 the children of Israel who had returned from Exile celebrated Passover with "all who had joined them and separated themselves from the pollutions of the nations of the land to worship the LORD, the God of Israel" (6:21). Historically these groups were not the same and may have been expelled for different reasons, but considered together they constitute a selected shaping of the community that punctuates chs. 1–6, which is the segment on the Return and the building of the Temple: of the first repatriates by YHWH, of the builders by the leaders, and then of an unsullied congregation by all the worshipers' choice.

Chapters 7–10 are also enveloped by acts of selection: YHWH has singled out Ezra in ch. 7: the good hand of YHWH is upon him. At the end of ch. 10 the whole people have themselves made a choice for YHWH. Unlike before (2:62 and 6:21), the commitment to the purity of the group no longer concerns just the cult, the Temple, and festival worship. Now it touches the heart of community: its family life and hence its future.

Marriage within one's group is called endogamy and marriage outside it exogamy. The question is open in Scripture. Early restrictions against intermarriage seem to have been to preserve tribal property and prerogative.[4] But Ezra does not discuss marriage in these terms.

The earlier chapters of Ezra–Nehemiah have argued the unbroken sovereignty of YHWH over history despite the tragedy of the Exile, and

---

[4] David Bossman, "Ezra's Marriage Reform: Israel Defined" *BTB* 9 (1979) 34.

over the Persians despite the Israelites' subjugation. Ezra the priest and
scribe has been presented as a unique embodiment of Israel's complex
religious heritage. Now Ezra–Nehemiah will show that faith in YHWH is
no abstract construction of reality: it is a demanding engagement with
life itself. Domestic life is at the center of any society's sense of itself and
its relation to the world. By insisting that the Judahites' family ties be
given over to YHWH Ezra is demanding the fullness of covenantal commitment. Community cannot be a matter of affection only, or of property
or clan alliances. The community's physical survival is not enough.

Speaking in the court of the Temple, Ezra sets the justice of YHWH
against the pollution of the land and the sinfulness of the people. The
holy otherness of YHWH is now to be mirrored by correlative qualities
in the people. Chapter 9 is central to the whole book because of its contrast between the way the people are and should be. As the people of
an earlier time had asked Samuel for a king to provide them with unity
and identity (1 Samuel 8), so now Ezra wants a new criterion of self-
definition for them. Here endogamy stands for something profound
about the people of Israel.

Ezra requires endogamy in order to imbue Israel with its lost sense
of self and continuity. This sense of rootedness used to come from the
Davidic dynasty's "royal seed," but we have seen how the dynasty's
incumbent, Zerubbabel, disappeared by the end of ch. 6. The Davidic
family was only second-ranked among the repatriates in ch. 8.

Now Israel's identity is to be carried by a "holy seed," the purified
people descended from the returned exiles. The priests had always
needed to be cultically pure, and Ezra declared them so after the fast
when he entrusted the Temple treasure to them (8:28). But now all the
people must be separated from blood contamination. The progressive
selections through Ezra 1–10 imply that YHWH's choice is always true:
of the first repatriates in ch. 1 and of Ezra in ch. 7. But the restored community cannot be molded and sanctified passively. Holiness will reside in those people who organize themselves pragmatically.

Ezra is not necessarily proposing a social program for all time: it is
an attempt to gain a "secure hold (lit. "peg") . . . a brief (or: a measure
of) revival in [their] slavery" (9:8). The intermarriages are called impure, but the foreign wives and children are not sinful. No blame is attached to them.

The theological point is this: Ezra is strengthening the Judahites to
live with the contradiction that exists between YHWH's promise of freedom in the land and their present subservience to foreign rulers. Here
is a holding-in-tension of present faithful acceptance and future aspiration. To do that the people must become as self-aware and commit-
ted as Ezra himself.

Rhetorical Situation

One cannot impose an identity on a people. Chapter 1 was about the changing relation of faith to power in the new world after the fall of Jerusalem. Now in ch. 10, just before the introduction of the governor Nehemiah, we see the limits of that relation. Ezra is gifted by God and empowered by the Persians, but no force can constrain a people to see themselves in a certain vision of things. They must be persuaded to adopt his idea if it is to achieve more than the immediate goal of banishing the foreign wives and children.

An added complexity is that the leaders themselves have intermarried: "And the hand of the chiefs and the officials was first in this unfaithfulness" (9:2). How does one affirm authority and bring deep social transformation yet denounce those leaders who have been abusing their position and introducing the wrong kind of change? In ch. 5 the Judahites had to bring the Persian ruler to a new decision on the Temple's construction without criticizing previous imperial policy. Here Ezra must bring to bear the authority of YHWH's Law without appearing to subordinate it to his civil power from the Persians.

In ch. 5 the repatriates had to use tact in their letter to the king. Now Ezra chooses to apply restraint in dealing with the people. The event occurs in the middle of the ninth month, presumably the first year of Ezra's mission. What had he been doing for the first four months, and had he not noticed the problem? As the text presents the matter he has to be informed of the intermarriages. He lets the crisis be addressed first by the sons of the Exile themselves.

Although we have seen that the prophetic tradition is maintained allusively in the language of the Book of Ezra we are far from the defiant condemnations of ruler and society by Israel's prophets like Elijah and Amos. This post-Exilic world is a place of principles realized through negotiations, strategies, and patience.

Rhetorical Strategies

Ezra does not speak imperiously or threateningly. Indeed, he does not speak to the Israelites at all in ch. 9. Conspicuously in a book with so much long discourse, Ezra at first says nothing. His quiet desolation dramatically appeals to the sensibilities of the repatriates while marking the limits of rhetoric. The community cannot be built on words alone.

Taken together the gestures of sitting silently on the ground and tearing one's hair and one's garment should be regarded as expressive of the rites of mourning for the dead, even though separately any one of them is performed in other contexts too.[5] Because of its sin the community deserves the judgment of death: "YHWH, God of Israel, righteous [are] you!" By acts of mourning for the death of the community Ezra demonstrates that he and the leaders who informed him accept this verdict. His first approach to the people is in solidarity with them and with the previous generations back to the "days of our fathers" (9:7). Ezra becomes a mediator with God in the face of the people's sin as Moses had been in Exodus 32 after the worship of the golden calf.

Chapter 7 introduced Ezra with an argumentation largely based on his "ethos" or character. Such kinds of persuasion normally involve "devices of communion" that build up the link between the audience and the orator. In this sense Ezra's ritual solidarity is consistent with his earlier presentation. He makes himself part of the context of the rhetorical situation and the communication act.

The gestures are ritualized and continue the attention of Ezra–Nehemiah to the role of worship in the restored society. As we have seen, it is one of the complexities of the book that Ezra the priest is not a Temple official, nor is he connected with the rebuilding of the Temple or its sacrifices. But his first words in ch. 7 are in the form of a psalm-blessing (v. 27), and upon arriving in Jerusalem his first action is to restore the Temple vessels. So too he first performs gestures of worship here. It is a classic penitential rite: first sitting on the ground in silence, then a confession of sin with the arms in the air, and a prayer of supplication.[6]

Rhetorical Devices

Ezra is not a full character in any narrative sense of one whose flaws and strengths resemble our own. He is a figurative ideal of the man of God. Some direct definitions have given us close knowledge of his virtues. He has "the good hand of his God upon him" and his "heart set to inquire [after] the Law of YHWH" (7:9-10). The Book of Ezra deepens our acquaintance with him by playing between narra-

[5] H. G. M. Williamson, *Ezra, Nehemiah* (Waco, Texas: Word Books, 1985) 132–33, in reference to Gen 37:34; 2 Sam 1:11; Job 1:20; 2:13; Mic 1:8; Isa 22:12; Jer 16:6; 41:5; Ezek 3:15; 7:18; 26:16.

[6] Luis Alonso-Schökel, *Cronicas, Esdras, Nehemias. Los Libros Sagrados* 6, eds. Luis Alonso-Schökel and Juan Mateos (Madrid: Ediciones Cristiandad, 1976) 143. See similar elements in Moses' actions in Exod 9:29, in 1 Kings 8, the Prayer of Solomon, and Isa 1:15, the vision of Isaiah.

tion in the first person and the third. Like Nehemiah later, Ezra is a memoirist, a genre unique to Ezra–Nehemiah in biblical narrative. Ezra's first-person account is in Ezra 7–10.[7]

The role of the "omniscient narrator" is curtailed just as YHWH himself remains behind the scene of the action. Ezra's understanding is devout but not supernatural. His portrayal relies heavily on the interactions between the narrator's point of view and his. We readers are invited to admire his qualities, among them reliability, but we are not dispensed from critical interpretation of his words. Just as the sons of the Exile must be participants in their own reformation, so we must be alert readers.

Ezra solves the rhetorical problems by choosing a certain kind of discourse and by using it to create associations and unities that preclude other solutions.

KIND OF DISCOURSE

He says a "sermon-prayer." As an address to YHWH it is rhetoric of the kind called deliberative, that is, speech as an attempt to persuade the listener to take some action in the future. It beseeches YHWH for help. Analyzed as public discourse it is also deliberative because the people overhear it and are swayed to a decision.

As explained in the Introduction, the other kinds of discourse are epideictic to praise or blame, and judicial to determine guilt or innocence. Ezra's prayer precludes the former because it is a prayer for forgiveness that presupposes sin and already accepts blame. He does not encourage the latter judicial type since, in his view of events, the exogamists are already judged guilty by YHWH and there is no need of further proof: "Behold us before you in our guilt" (9:15).

His argument against the foreign families creates a dissociation or severance in his construct of reality between YHWH and the people: his assumption that the people are blameworthy correlatively exonerates YHWH. The people are far from YHWH because of their sin. Nor may the Israelites plead ignorance of the Law. The only questions are whether the people will again break the commandments of God (9:14), and whether God will mercifully punish them less than they deserve (9:13).

---

[7] Some would further add Nehemiah 8 or 9–10 or all of these. This commentary does not interpret these chapters as part of a first-person account for reasons discussed in the chapter on those passages. They may have the Memoir among their sources.

ASSOCIATION OF EZRA, THE AUDIENCE, AND GOD

This is an argument based less on logic than on the emotion of the audience and the authority of the speaker. Part of his rhetorical solution is to associate his prayer with the people's situation in such a way that their action is the only answer to his prayer.[8] Other solutions than this are made to seem repugnant or irreverent. Ezra prays for divine mercy. Either YHWH will not have heard the prayer, in which case he has abandoned them and they are doomed, or he does hear the prayer, in which case they are openly defying him if they continue the forbidden marriages. By addressing YHWH only Ezra effectively makes the Israelites accountable for the consequences of their own faith. His strategy is simply to pray as a good Israelite, and the burden of response rests on those who overhear him. Thus in 10:8 the people will gather to hear him according to the "advice of the chiefs and the elders," not by his order or the word of the Law.

Without detailed recourse to the Law a legal problem is handled by public prayer and cultic gesture. Otherwise the point could be argued juridically and Ezra would have to consider the conditions that led to the intermarriages. "We have abandoned your commandments which you commanded through your slaves the prophets" (9:10-11). No biblical prophet actually condemns intermarriage, as we will see. As in ch. 7 Ezra is again a figure around whom the language of the prophetic, the legal, and the cultic traditions freely blend.

Ezra does not try to demonstrate that YHWH is with Israel. His question poses a rhetorical dilemma and implies that they must prove that truth themselves by their action: "Shall we again break your commandments and marry into the peoples of these abominations?" (9:14). If the people continue to marry foreigners they are answering "yes" to the question. If they stop the intermarriages they are admitting their current sinfulness and YHWH's rightful sovereignty over them. Ezra says simply, "YHWH, God of Israel, righteous [are] you! Yet we are left an escaped remnant as this day" (9:15). The people must affirm or deny their cooperation with his faith by reaching a decision about their family life.

Ezra need not cite personal experience since his remarks are a prayer made to the all-knowing God. This "prayer rhetoric" keeps the primary emphasis on his relationship with YHWH while building his relationship with the people. It continues to establish his character as in ch. 7. It does so now in response to their remarks and in continuing

---

[8] The technical term for an address made to one audience but with another also in mind is *percontatio.*

relation to YHWH. Future arguments can thus be "arguments of the person" of the type: "We know him, so it must be so."[9]

UNITIES OF AUDIENCE, TIME, AND TORAH TRADITION

Ezra's "sermon-prayer" creates an interconnection of ideas that rhetorically impels the Israelites toward his position on the issues of leadership, authority, and community.

First, by praying he promotes unity among the audience, since no Israelites should object to a prayer, whatever their own opinions about exogamy. Using the first person, he unites himself to the audience as a fellow sinner pleading with them for forgiveness: "My God, I am ashamed . . . for our iniquities have increased . . . ." By addressing YHWH in their hearing he also joins the people and YHWH into one audience, linking them rhetorically as the Law does authoritatively.

We have seen how sequential time in the book is blurred in a projection of events that is theologically structured.[10] Here Ezra creates a unity of time in at least two ways. First, in his paraphrase of Scripture prophets of the past give imperatives for the present: ". . . we have abandoned your commandments which you commanded through your slaves, the prophets, saying, ' . . . your daughters—do not give [them] to their sons and their daughters—do not take [them] for your sons'" (v. 11). What was preached formerly must be performed now, even though times and circumstances have changed. Second, the audience's present trouble is related to their past misdeeds in such a way that future sins will surely lead to new woes: "Shall we again break your commandments and marry into the peoples of these abominations?" (v. 14).

Last, Ezra implies a neat and united Torah tradition. His allusions to "[YHWH's] slaves, the prophets" (v. 11) are a free pastiche of various books,[11] the distinction between Law and prophecy being overridden by subsuming "the whole under the category of the spoken, prophetic word of God."[12] In fact, as we mentioned, the Torah is not univocal on the issue of foreign marriages. We will see later how his paraphrasing of the biblical tradition is faithful but idiosyncratic and construable.

---

[9] Olivier Reboul, *La rhétorique* (5th ed. Paris: Presses Universitaires de France, 1996) 181.

[10] See "Present Eschatology" in the treatment of chs. 5–6 and "Ezra and the Past, Present, and Future" in the discussion of ch. 7.

[11] Deut 7:1-3; 11:8; 23:4-9; 2 Kings 21:16; Isa 1:19.

[12] Williamson, *Ezra, Nehemiah* 137. See also his 161.

These rhetorically-created associations are set against two distinctions and separations. Contrasting with Ezra's solidarity with the people are the wives' foreignness and the Israelites' resulting separation from YHWH. Much of the emphasis of the chapter is in the repeated contrast between YHWH who is gracious and righteous and the disobedient Israelites whose perversity is so amply described. By implication the Israelites' divorce from the foreigners would help join them to YHWH.

Arrangement

Only after the celebration of Passover "in joy" (6:22) does Ezra begin the rites of mourning. The predominance of joy is the appropriate order for any reception of the Law. And, like the ceremonies that mark all important events in the book, this one has a communal aspect.

When Ezra finally speaks, form-critically his remarks are unique.[13] The sequence here is: a general confession including a penitential lament (vv. 6-7), mention of YHWH's present mercies (vv. 8-9), a specific confession (vv. 10-12), a statement of future intent (vv. 13-14), and a concluding general confession (v. 15). But it asks nothing of YHWH: it has no supplication to him in the imperative or jussive. Instead, in 9:12 Ezra turns to the people and pleads with them: "And now your daughters—do not give [them] to their sons and their daughters—do not take [them] for your sons. And do not inquire after their welfare and good ever." This distinguishes the sequence from penitential psalms of lament and from other comparable passages like Neh 1:5-11 and 9:6-28. The omission implies that YHWH has already shown the fullness of mercy and a response is due from the people.

In the case of this prayer the sequence of much Greco-Latin rhetoric is a helpful tool for analysis. The first part of a classic deliberative discourse is the introduction or *exordium*.[14] In it the speaker seeks the good will of the audience by establishing three realities: some sort of relation with the audience, an attitude toward the subject, and some sense of oneself, what kind of person one is or chooses to be thought to be. The speaker must define himself or herself and the problem.

Ezra's silent action of tearing his garment and beard and sitting dumbfounded until the evening sacrifice effectively begins the exordium. Chapter 7 has already gone far in presenting his general character. The subject at hand is the iniquity of the people and their chiefs,

---

[13] Ibid. 128.

[14] Also called "proem": George A. Kennedy, *New Testament Interpretation through Rhetorical Criticism* (Chapel Hill and London: University of North Carolina Press, 1984) 48.

to be described figuratively and hyperbolically: "our iniquities have increased to over [our] head[s] and our guilt has grown to the skies." He immediately establishes this matter as shameful and himself as deeply and piously affected.

He finally gives voice to his symbolic actions in v. 6: "My God, I am ashamed and mortified to raise, my God, my face to you." His relation with the audience is solidary; his attitude toward the iniquity is repentant; he projects an image of devotion and drama. He is at one with the audience, who are "all those who tremble at the word of the God of Israel on account of the unfaithfulness of the Exile" (v. 3). His self-definition is achieved lexically ("ashamed," "mortified") and grammatically ("our").

The body of the discourse is in vv. 7-9. It begins with a *narratio*, a description of the background of the event.[15] First Ezra recalls past events ("anamnesis") as he traces the history of YHWH's favor and the people's unfaithfulness. He gives no latitude for the special circumstances of the Babylonian invasion, and implicitly treats the intermarriages as a cause of the Exilic confusion rather than its effect ("metonymy"): "And because of our iniquities, we, our kings, [and] our priests have been given into the hand of kings of the lands, to the sword, to captivity, to pillage, and to open shame (lit. "shame of face"), as this day" (9:7).

The next part of the body is the argumentation, the *confirmatio* or central part of the whole speech. In it Ezra makes the categorical proposition that the present moment is an occasion of grace, and he proposes the best response: "But now for a brief moment there has been favor from YHWH our God to leave us an escaped remnant . . . to give us revival, to erect the house of our God and to restore (lit. "set up") its ruins and to give us a fence in Judah and in Jerusalem" (9:8-9).[16]

His argument is quasi-logical here, of the kind called "*secundum quid.*" That is, since something is generally true, therefore it is true in a highly specialized class. YHWH wants Israel to be pure; therefore they must put aside even their impure wives and children.

He substitutes a part for the whole ("synecdoche"). In his argument here the foreign wives stand for all impurity, and purity is one's whole response to YHWH.

"What can we say, our God, after this?" (9:10). Ezra then answers his own question with another proof: the prophets are brought to bear as witnesses (9:11-12).[17] He increases his projected self-image of humil-

---

[15] Ibid. 68.

[16] Assuring someone of something is called "asphalia": ibid. 17

[17] This kind of proof is technically called *argumentum ad verecundiam*, an appeal to reverence to authority, and *apomnemonysis*, quotation of an approved authority.

ity by subordinating his own remarks to those of others. The faithful servant-prophets who passed on the commands of YHWH are set against the errant chiefs and the people who followed them.

Verse 13 concludes the *confirmatio* with a repetition that forms an envelope figure with v. 8 around the main body of the prayer: God has given the people an escape. In closing the *confirmatio* Ezra also amplifies it, for despite all their iniquity mounting over their heads to the skies YHWH is punishing them less than they deserve.

Then follows the *peroratio* (vv. 14-15). The purpose of a *peroratio* is often to recapitulate the *confirmatio* and make a final emotional appeal. Ezra speaks here in virtue of the anger of YHWH and invokes the response of fear and self-blame: "Shall we again break your commandments? . . . Shall you not be angry with us [to the point of] destroying . . . ?" One wonders if "escaped remnant" in v. 15 has not come to mean an escape not from Exile now but from the deserved wrath of YHWH.

The conclusion, v. 15, is short. In this stage a rhetor will typically restate the thesis, make emotional appeals, incite to action, and confirm the arguments of an exaggerated character. Ezra achieves each of those goals.

The restatement of the thesis is the exclamation: "YHWH, God of Israel, righteous [are] you!" Divine righteousness has been the essence of Ezra's argument. The incitement to action is the appeal that YHWH look on the people in their iniquity: "Behold us before you in our guilt." The implication for the Israelites is that they too should present themselves to YHWH.

The various stages of the argument are bound together and given a patina of logicality by repetitions of *kî*, a Hebrew particle meaning variously "because," "although," "yet," "indeed." (See the Literal Translation.)

When Ezra speaks again, and for the last time in this episode, he urges the people to "give thanks to YHWH . . . do his will and be separated from the peoples of the land . . ." (10:10). This sequence—confession of guilt and thanks, submission and action—is the natural one in the order of conversion and restoration. It recalls Ezra's own description: he first "set his heart to inquire [after] the Law of YHWH" and only then "to act upon [it] and to teach [it] in Israel" (7:10).

As outlined in the Introduction, the events here end the second movement of the book and close, like the others, with a liturgical celebration: in 10:19 the people sacrifice a ram.

Answering one's own questions is called *subjectio*. See Kennedy, *New Testament Interpretation* 16, 94, and 123.

Vocabulary

The leaders of the community come to Ezra and list the peoples with whom the Israelites, the "holy seed," have intermingled. This is a deliberate allusion to Deut 7:1-6, which also lists several peoples and mentions the "holy nation." But the list in Ezra has added to that of Deuteronomy the names of the Ammonites, the Moabites, and the Egyptians, who are never among the rosters of the native Canaanites. The Ammonites, in fact, were contemporary enemies of the repatriates and these three peoples are forbidden to enter the "congregation of YHWH" in Deut 23:4-9. In other words the list in Ezra 9 is a midrashic conflation of two passages in Deuteronomy.[18]

Ezra also interweaves the same two Deuteronomy texts in 9:11-12. His mention of "the land which you are going in to possess," is close to Deut 7:1, and his plea that the people not inquire after their welfare and good ever is a fairly exact citation of Deut 23:6 [MT 7].

The expulsion of the foreigners is thus given a midrashic justification through blended biblical allusions made by both Ezra and the chiefs. But the chiefs begin them in their first comments to Ezra, although he is the skilled scribe. In other words, they are made to show some of his expertise just as he has mourned for their sin, and so they together demonstrate verbally the solidarity needed to undertake action.

Again, as in the vocabulary of ch. 7, the language of the Exodus and Conquest motifs and of the prophetic heritage are attached to Ezra's mission, but with a twist of meaning that advances his new purposes. The peoples have "intermingled," using a verb that is related to the "mixed multitude" who leave Egypt in Exod 12:38. The same verb occurs elsewhere in the sense of intermarriage only in Ps 106:35, a psalm of contrition with reference again to the Exodus and the sinfulness of the people after the capture of the land.[19] The exact phrase "holy seed" occurs elsewhere only in Isa 6:13. There it refers to the remnant who stayed in the land, in Ezra to the returned exiles. In Exod 19:5-7 YHWH tells Moses that the people who had just escaped Egypt will be a "kingdom of priests and a holy nation" if they heed his words. They will be "priests of YHWH" and a "blessed seed" in Isa 61:6, 9. But unlike these passages the Book of Ezra sees no future day when all the people will be priests. Ezra cannot stand before YHWH, and he urges the people to

[18] Michael Fishbane, *Biblical Interpretation in Ancient Israel* (Oxford: Clarendon Press, 1985) 115–21.

[19] In *hitpael* the five other occurrences are 2 Kings 18:23; Isa 36:8; Prov 14:10; 20:19; 24:21, where it means variously "to wager," "to disobey," "to share" (joys), "to associate" (with fools).

make confession or literally to "give thanks." The only other occurrence of this verbal phrase is in Josh 7:19. There Joshua falls to the ground and bemoans the sin of the people and their defeat at the hands of the Amorites, the Canaanites, and all the inhabitants of the land, saying as Ezra does here about intermarriage with them: "O Lord, what can I say after [these events]?" (Josh 7:8; cf. Ezra 9:10).

The Response to Ezra's Speech

Shecaniah's first response to Ezra goes against the intention of Ezra's prayer. Ezra had prayed that the Israelites themselves would take repentant action. Shecaniah instead gives the initiative back to Ezra: "'Arise! for on you [rests] the matter. And we [will be] with you. Be strong and act!'" (10:4). He suggests a pact "according to the Law" but does nothing to arrange one.[20]

In turn Ezra reacts to Shecaniah by self-effacement. His first-person memoir ends; the narration in ch. 10 is now back in the third person. He makes the assembly swear to act "according to this word"—which word and whose is ambiguous. He leaves them and goes off to fast and mourn in a private room (10:6).

His departure brings others to action. "They" send word for the repatriates to gather (10:7). Delinquents will be punished "according to the advice of the chiefs and the elders," not by the order of Ezra.

As Ezra shrinks his rhetorical presence the number of Israelites in attendance grows continually. First the chiefs see him fall down in mourning (9:1). Then the God-fearers join him and them: "all who trembled at the words of the God of Israel on account of the unfaithfulness of the Exile" (9:3). During his public prayer he is overheard and imitated by "a very large crowd from Israel . . . men and women and children" (10:1). (It is a measure of the gravity of the crisis and the crowd's size that, unusually for Scripture, it is said to include women and children.) Then he takes the oath of "the chiefs of the priests, the Levites, and all Israel" (10:5). Finally "all the men of Judah and Benjamin" (10:9) comprise the last assembly.

This full audience is "shaking on [account of] the matter and the rains" like the smaller circle of pious men who had first trembled at the words of YHWH. The similar actions of trembling and shaking demonstrate the growing cohesion of the audience in the course of its persuasion, and hence Ezra's success. It reinforces the links between the

---

[20] In this light it is best to read 10:3 as "according to the counsel of my lord," meaning Ezra rather than YHWH. The Masoretic text is a pious correction.

first audience of social and religious leaders and the general assembly that gathers for his second speech.

The first measure the community takes is the general order that the audience be increased again: anyone who does not come will be punished (10:8). After his prayer, when Ezra finally addresses the people, it is the final and largest audience that hears him. They have already been weeping, like him (10:1).

When Ezra does finally speak again it is explicitly as a priest (10:10) and directly to the people rather than to YHWH. He briefly summarizes his remarks from ch. 9, changing them from a prayer to a direct exhortation.[21] He calls the people unfaithful, then orders them to make confession to God, to do the divine will, and to separate themselves from the foreigners. The Hebrew for "to make confession" implies all that Ezra said in his first speech about repentance and deliverance. It is praise rendered by admitting and abandoning sin.[22]

After Ezra's second intervention not just Shecaniah but all the people speak up. The opposition is named, but they do not hold matters up. The children of the Exile acknowledge their responsibility for action as Ezra wanted them to: "According to your word [it is] upon us to do!" (10:13).

Ezra does not speak again in the text. With unrecorded words he chooses family heads, but it is they who investigate and reach decisions. The exogamists put aside their foreign wives and children.

Ezra's speech finally achieves its goal through a complement of strategic taciturnity. Silence balances discourse in the chapters just as concurrence with the speaker Ezra must be matched by initiative in the audience, the community. By acting ritually, then speaking then keeping silent again Ezra is marking the boundary of oral persuasion and the relativity of human leadership. The implied antithesis to these limits is the sovereignty of YHWH whose will they finally do "according to the Law" (10:3, 11).

Chapter 10 ends with a names list genealogically arranged. The reinstated Temple vessels provided continuity in the worship in ch. 7. Now, as the people shape their domestic future, the lines of family descent that envelop this episode at the end of chs. 8 and 10 work, like the liturgy, as an instrument of connectedness with the past, a motif

---

[21] The technical term is *commoratio*, repetition of the same thought. See Richard A. Lanham, *A Handlist of Rhetorical Terms. A Guide for Students of English Literature* (Berkeley: University of California Press, 1968) 32.

[22] See Williamson, *Ezra, Nehemiah* 155 for details: "Just as in ascribing praise to God the worshipper is perforce accepting his own sinfulness and God's judgment upon it, so conversely to express that acceptance openly glorified God as the righteous judge."

that runs throughout the book. Therefore it ends too with a liturgical celebration, like each of the three units of building projects. In 10:19 the people sacrifice a ram.

Conclusion

Key to Ezra's theology is the question of how to dialogue fruitfully with the world. Israel must accept Persian political overlords, but Ezra demands that it reconstitute itself by its own rule of faith. The adaptability of this rule of faith is finite. It cannot be adjusted simply according to good will. Changes imposed from the outside—like the Exile—are not enough.

Israel is blessed and all the tribes of the world will still be blessed in it (Gen 12:3) but only in the measure that Israel is still Israel. YHWH gives "favor" (9:8) but Israel must be true to itself to know that grace. Ezra is implying that Israel's identity is bound up with its experience of the covenant and its ability to recall and celebrate it. By demanding endogamy Ezra is asking Israel to recognize the pragmatic limits of its receptivity to grace.

This is the end of Zechariah's vision of Jerusalem "inhabited as villages without walls" and Second Isaiah's vision of Israel as a "light to the nations."[23] Their pragmatism was also a corrective to the tendency of some apocalyptic circles to withdraw from the community to await YHWH's final act of vindication.[24]

In the text as it stands the altar and the Temple are rebuilt first, and the theology of the Temple is the angle of observation on the futher events of the Restoration. The Temple is already rebuilt because the community cannot change without liturgy, the link to the past that keeps memory alive. Ezra creates the response to the Law before he actually proclaims the Law: he does not read the Law in order to reform the people. Rather, it is the reformed people to whom the Law is read.[25] Later, in Nehemiah 8, he will be able to read the Law to the acclaim of

---

[23] Zech 2:4 [MT 2:9] and Isa 49:6.

[24] See Jean-Marie van Cangh, "Temps et eschatologie dans l'Ancient Testament," *Temps et eschatologie: données bibliques et problématiques contemporaines*, ed. Jean-Louis Leuba (Paris: Cerf, 1994) 17–38, who uses Jacques Vermeylen's analysis of three schools of eschatology in the Old Testament. One of them is "future passive eschatology" as in P, Second and Third Isaiah, Haggai, Joel, and Proto-Zechariah. Everything comes according to a plan fixed by God. Humanity must wait patiently for God to bring about a better future.

[25] Williamson, *Ezra and Nehemiah* 1.

the assembly because now he prays in such a way that they will be able to see the connection between it and their lives. His full achievement will hence be to exalt the Law but also to set it in context as the fruit and agency of one's lived relation with YHWH, guided and celebrated by worship.

Thus Ezra's first achievement is not administrative but rhetorical. Through his discourse and silence he presents himself to the people, but also the people to God. He achieves this goal before pronouncing the Law because, he implies, the Law requires a community to receive it, and any true community must be rooted in self-understanding, prayer, and worship. Ezra never presents the issue in terms of preserving Israelite property. Safeguarding the land is no longer the point. The holiness of the people must come before that of the land, and any modern nation forgets that at its peril.

Ezra is not a messenger from God like the classical prophets, but it is fitting that tradition calls him a "lawgiver" like Moses.[26] He becomes a mediator with YHWH in the face of the people's sin as Moses had been in Exodus 32 after the sin with the golden calf. But for Ezra participation in the fellowship of believers precedes understanding of its Law. Language always has to do with social environment. As Northrop Frye says, "We belong to something before we are anything. . . . Our loyalties and sense of solidarity are prior to intelligence."[27] So too Ezra moves the audience to concur with him as a rhetor before they obey him as a leader. His authority does not derive from their consent: it was given him by the Persians. He is presented as united with YHWH, allied with the king, and coherent within himself and within history. He could have spoken in imperative, performative language as the king had in ch. 4: "And the king gave him—according to the hand of YHWH his God upon him—all he requested" (7:6). But he wants his leadership to be planted in the soil of their common concern because responsibility in the new Israel must be a common task.

Ezra leads the people by leading them in prayer. The precedence of prayer is set as the precondition for the true reception of the Law. He is exalting the Law but also relativizing it as dependent on or an outgrowth of personal relationship with YHWH. Similarly, fitting social

[26] According to Shemaryahu Talmon, "Ezra and Nehemiah," *The Literary Guide to the Bible*, eds. Robert Alter and Frank Kermode (Cambridge, Mass.: Harvard University Press, 1987) 357, the Jewish sages call Ezra a second Moses, equal to him in worth. The Decalogue would have been revealed to him except that Moses lived before him.

[27] Northrop Frye, *Words with Power. Being a Second Study of "The Bible and Literature"* (San Diego, New York, and London: Harcourt Brace Jovanovich, 1990) 17.

relations must be established by reference to one's right relation with God. Holiness must now reside in the people. It is not just a matter for the cult and priests. Israel's peoplehood must be defined by its collective responsibility and holiness, as in Exod 19:6.

At the same time, a community is not constituted simply to rest in itself. It is not enough to form a fellowship for its own sake. No people can avoid questions of content: after Egypt must come Sinai. That is, the formation of the Israelites in the Exodus must be followed by the gift and responsibility of the Law at Mount Sinai.

An idea of Walter Brueggemann's is pertinent: the central question in the Bible is not "emancipation but rootage, not meaning but belonging, not isolation from others but placement between the generation of promise and fulfillment."[28]

Ezra's concern about mixed marriages is also based on the often-neglected truth that the family is not ideologically neutral. The way we shape the smallest cell of our society will affect the whole. The home is part of the realm of faith, and the actions of our daily domestic life must be taken seriously.

In spite of all the threats of seizure of property and excommunication the campaign to exclude foreigners only brought about 113 divorces (10:18-43). The text is so theologically constructed that we are not expected to worry about the foreign women and children as full characters. We are not meant to ask what their reactions and their fate were. No other solution than expulsion is sought because the rhetorical problem is not the mixed marriages in themselves but their significance in a theological context. In the same way we do not know why the people of the land were forbidden to build the Temple in ch. 4. The dismissal of the wives for the sake of the purity of society is a theological argument from finality. The text breaks off: it is not clear that the infractors actually carried out the banishment. Like the presentation of Ezra himself, the foreigners stand principally for theological realities, whatever the historicity of their existence.

Ezra's intervention in the family life of the Israelites is the stimulus for the exploration of the dynamic between leadership and community, faith and law, prayer and action, speech and silence.

---

[28] Walter Brueggemann, *The Land. Place as Gift, Promise and Challenge in Biblical Faith*. Overtures to Biblical Theology 1, eds. Walter Brueggemann and John R. Donahue (Philadelphia: Fortress, 1977) 187.

1:1   The words of Nehemiah the son of Hacaliah.
Now it happened in the month of Kislev,
in the twentieth year,
as I was in Susa the capital (or: citadel?),

1:2   that Hanani, one of my brethren, came with [certain] men
from Judah;
and I asked them about the Jews,
the remnant,
who had escaped (lit. "remained from," "survived") captivity,
and about Jerusalem.

1:3   And they said to me,
"The survivors (lit. "those who remained") there in the
province
who escaped (lit. "remained from") captivity
are in great trouble (lit. "evil")
and shame;
and the wall of Jerusalem is breached,
and its gates are gutted (lit. "eaten") by fire."

1:4   When I heard these words
I sat down
and wept,
and mourned for days;
and I continued fasting
and praying before the God of the heavens.

1:5   And I said,
"Please, YHWH, God of the heavens,
the great and fearsome God
who keeps covenant
and lovingkindness with those who love him
and keep his commandments;

1:6   let your ear be attentive,
and your eyes open, to hear the prayer of your slave
which I now pray before you now (lit. "today") day and
night on [behalf of] the sons of Israel your slaves,
confessing the sins of the sons of Israel,
which we have sinned against you.
Indeed (or: including, even), I and my father's house have
sinned.

1:7   We have acted very unfaithfully (or: corruptly) against you,
and have not kept the commandments,

the statutes,
and the ordinances
which you commanded your slave Moses.

1:8   Remember the word
which you commanded your slave Moses,
saying,
'If you are unfaithful (or: betraying)
I will scatter you among the peoples;

1:9   but if you return to me
and keep my commandments
and do them,
though your dispersed [people] are at the farthest horizon
    (lit. "edge of the skies," or "heavens"),
I will gather them from there
and bring them to the place
which I have chosen,
to make my name inhabit there.'

1:10   They are your slaves
and your people,
whom you have redeemed by your great power
and by your strong hand.

1:11   O Lord, let your ear be attentive to the prayer of your slave,
and to the prayer of your slaves
who delight (or: want) to fear your name;
and give success to your slave today,
and give him mercy in the sight of this man."
And I was cupbearer to the king.

2:1   In the month of Nisan, in the twentieth year of King
    Artaxerxes,
[when] wine [was] before him,
I took up the wine
and gave it to the king.
Now I had not (or: had never) been sad (lit. "evil") in his
    presence (lit. "before him").

2:2   And the king said to me,
"Why is your face sad (lit. "evil"), seeing you are not sick?
This is nothing else but sadness (lit. "evil") of the heart."
[Then] I was very much afraid.

2:3   I said to the king,
"May the king live for ever!
Why should my face not be sad (lit. "evil"),
when the city,
the place (lit. "house") of my fathers' sepulchres,

lies waste,
and its gates have been destroyed (lit. "eaten") by fire?"

2:4   Then the king said to me,
"For what do you make request?"
So I prayed to the God of the heavens.

2:5   And I said to the king,
"If it pleases (lit. "is good for") the king,
and if your slave is agreeable (lit. "good") in your sight
      (lit. "before you"),
[I request] that you send me to Judah,
to the city of my fathers' sepulchres,
that I may rebuild it."

2:6   And the king said to me
—the consort sitting beside him—
"How long will your journey last,
and when will you return?"
So it pleased (lit. "was good before") the king to send me;
and I gave him a time.

2:7   And I said to the king,
"If it pleases (lit. "is good for") the king,
let them give me letters to the governors of the province
      Beyond the River,
that they may let me cross
until I come to Judah;

2:8   and a letter to Asaph,
the keeper of the king's forest,
that he may give me timber to make beams for the gates of
      the temple fortress,
for the city wall,
and for the house
which I shall occupy (lit. "come to it")."
And the king granted me what I asked,
for the good hand of my God was upon me.

2:9   Then I came to the governors of the province Beyond
      the River,
and gave them the king's letters.
Now the king had sent with me the army officers
      (or: chiefs)
and horsemen.

2:10   But when Sanballat
the Horonite
and Tobiah
the slave,

the Ammonite, heard this,
it displeased them (lit. "did evil to them") greatly
that some one had come to seek the good of the sons of Israel.

2:11   So I came to Jerusalem
and was there three days.

2:12   Then I arose in the night, I and a few men with me;
and I did not tell anyone
what my God had put into my heart to do for Jerusalem.
There was no beast with me but the beast on which I rode.

2:13   I went out by the Valley Gate by night to the Dragon Well
   and to the Dung Gate,
and I inspected (?) the walls of Jerusalem
which were breached
and its gates had been destroyed (lit. "eaten") by fire.

2:14   And I crossed to the Fountain Gate and to the King's Pool;
but there was no place for the beast under me to pass.

2:15   Then I went up by the stream in the night
and inspected (?) the wall;
and I turned back (lit "returned")
and came (in) by the Valley Gate,
and so returned.

2:16   And the officials did not know
where I had gone
or what I was doing;
and the Jews,
the priests,
the nobles,
the officials,
and the rest
[that were] to do the work
I had hitherto not told.

2:17   Then I said to them,
"You see the trouble (lit. "evil") that we are in,
that Jerusalem [lies] waste
and its gates are gutted (lit. "eaten") by fire.
Come (lit. "go"),
let us build the wall of Jerusalem,
that we may no longer suffer (lit. "be") disgrace."

2:18   And I told them [of] the hand of my God
which was good upon me,
and also [of] the words of the king
which he had spoken to me.
And they said,

"Let us rise up
and build!"
So they strengthened their hands for the good.

2:19 But when Sanballat the Horonite
and Tobiah the slave, the Ammonite,
and Geshem the Arab heard of it,
they derided us
and despised us
and said,
"What is this thing
that you are doing?
Are you rebelling against the king?"

2:20 And I replied (lit. "returned a word") to them,
"The God of heaven, he will make us prosper,
and we his slaves will rise up and build;
but to you
there will be no portion or right or memorial in Jerusalem."

Chapter Six

NEHEMIAH 1–2

Introduction

The story lines thus far have run on the same broad course. Three projects have been authorized by a Persian king. They began in Exile and culminated in Jerusalem. The building—of the altar and the Temple, of the community itself and of the walls—has been the task of three groups and characters, each prepared in Exile and implemented in Judah by the medium of documents despite conflict.[1] Each renovation ends in a solemn celebration, the one here being delayed until Nehemiah 8 for reasons we will see then. Each unit is discrete, progressing without overt acknowledgment of its predecessors, but the vocabulary and argumentation make the allusions that the plot ignores.

We have already seen in previous chapters how these similarities point to the book's thematic development. Now comes one of the most important moments in Ezra–Nehemiah, the introduction of the second principal character. Nehemiah's commanding voice is added to this intricate pattern of recurrence and reverberation.

The narrative here is set in the same month as the last chapter and under a king also named Artaxerxes,[2] but it is weak historical glue and

---

[1] Tamara C. Eskenazi, *In an Age of Prose. A Literary Approach to Ezra–Nehemiah* (Atlanta, Ga.: Scholars, 1988) 4. Victor (Avigdor) Hurowitz, *I Have Built You an Exalted House: Temple Building in the Bible in Light of Mesopotamian and Northwest Semitic Writing* (Sheffield: Sheffield Academic Press, 1992) 64, says this resembles the pattern of the typical account of a building project in the ancient Near East.

[2] The month of Kislev in Neh 1:1 and Ezra 10:17. Many of the problems of dating stem from the texts' failure to specify if they mean Artaxerxes I (reigned 464–424) or II (reigned 404–359). Compare Ezra 4:6; 7:1; 8:1 and Neh 1:1. Sara Japhet, "Composition and Chronology in the Book of Ezra–Nehemiah," *Second Temple Studies: 2. Temple and Community in the Persian Period*, JSOT.S 175 (Sheffield: JSOT Press, 1994) 207: "There is no chronological structure that can be verified in historical-political terms."

there are no syntactical links. Nehemiah 1 makes no direct reference to earlier episodes at all: Nehemiah hears of the distress of the Judahites as though it were unrelieved. He is stricken with sadness, and mourns and prays. As an important official in the Persian court, he dares to seek the King's leave for a mission to rebuild Jerusalem. With all the necessary authority he journeys there, but at first he is taciturn about his plans. Like Ezra he waits three days (Ezra 8:32; Neh 2:11). Then he easily stirs the Judahites to rebuild the city walls. He confidently rebukes his foreign adversaries.

Rhetorical Situation

It is not clear if the walls are down because of a recent attack or since the beginning of the Return: in Ezra 4 the enemies had exaggerated their report of the walls being rebuilt then. They said that the walls were already being built when it was only the Temple. In any case the emphasis is not on some outside danger but on the shame of the Judahites who must live among such dilapidation. If the problem were entirely the breaches in the walls the people would not need a newcomer to get them repaired. In rhetorical terms the walls are simply the *topos* or "topic." A rhetorical "topic" is a "place" where the speaker looks for something to say about the subject of real interest. The walls are the lever that opens up a further set of problems in the matter of Israel's social and spiritual upbuilding.

Zerubbabel's legacy was to shape the independent identity of the Judahites by keeping the people of the land from the rebuilding of the Temple in Ezra 4. Ezra advanced it again by excluding foreigners from the family, but a distinct and pure community for its own sake will ultimately be empty. So will its worship. Purification is an act of religious obedience and social cohesion, not a goal in itself. One cannot have a community or a cult, even a pure one, without a setting in life and a pragmatic program of responsibility. During the reconstruction of the altar and the Temple in Ezra 3–4 the rhetoric asserted that identity and mission are joined. The negotiated concern for the family in Ezra 9 created the cohesive social environment for the peoplehood of the Judahites and their eventual reception of the Law. Nehemiah's material task is now to give architectural form to this polity. The chapters' deeper task is to separate the collective mission from any one personality or leadership, and to extend the covenant commitment on which it is founded beyond the immediate circle of Nehemiah's fellow citizens.

The order of these steps is significant. The place to worship is built first. That is, the beginning of the work precedes the attention to questions of right relations and structure. In the life of faith issues of context are not paramount, and they need not be fully resolved before any other action is undertaken, but neither are they dissociated from the larger principles to which the book links them by all the intertextual references we have been seeing.

We said in the last chapter that Exodus must be followed by Sinai in the sense that an experience of freedom cannot stand alone with no entailing commitments. Now comes, as it were, the Entry into the Land, the settling into a space in which the community can further know itself and soon hear the Law. One cannot wander forever. Freedom cannot mean aimlessness. Religious commitment in Ezra–Nehemiah involves not a detachment from the lived environment but a turning to it within the limits of the practical.

Persian sovereignty is beyond question. But after a "home" for YHWH in the Temple one should be built for the people. The discussion about intermarriage showed the importance of reformed domestic life within the covenant. Now the renovation of the material surroundings is described in the same narrative pattern under a different kind of leader.

Israel's boundaries—in its family life and urban space—are a mark of its reliance on YHWH alone. Any circumference of the society is relative to the depth of its commitment. Nehemiah 1–2 implies that the children of the Exile must have a degree of independence from their own leaders as well. Ezra was introduced as a figurative ideal of the man of God with "the good hand of his God upon him" and his "heart set to inquire [after] the law of YHWH" (7:9-10). But lest his silences and the diffident rhetoric of his prayer had not been enough to keep the Judahites from overreliance on him, he is now replaced altogether. Nehemiah suddenly appears, a man with no other warrant than his smooth tongue and his collection of Persian dispatches.

Like Ezra's mission, Nehemiah's here prepares for the reading of the Law in Nehemiah 8 and is fulfilled in it. In ch. 7 Artaxerxes did as Ezra willed, while Ezra was ordered to appoint judges to administer the law of Persia "according to the wisdom of [his] God" (7:25). This dialectic between the civic and the sacred continues in the succession of the royal cupbearer to the Torah sage. Nehemiah's counterfoil to Ezra makes clear the principle that Israel's faith is not dependent on an individual, however admirable. At the same time the tradition can be engaged in a new way that is hopeful, despite the disasters of Israel's history.

Form

Nehemiah speaks here in his own words, in an autobiographical memoir that is almost unique in Scripture. With Ezra's, the Memoirs of

Nehemiah are the only continuous account of a person's career written autobiographically in the Hebrew Bible. It continues from Nehemiah 1 to 7 with parts of chapters 12–13 and possibly 10–11.[3] From a rhetorical-critical perspective it is worthwhile to study how he manages the information and presents not only his own argument but also his audience's response to it.

In his Memoirs Nehemiah quotes his prayers to YHWH, his own words to those around him, and theirs to him. We who hear or read the Memoirs now constitute the third audience. The Book of Ezra also had multiple audiences. We in our day read the letters in Ezra 4 exchanged between the people of the land and the king. There the effect was to split the audiences: what enhanced the people in the king's eyes diminished them in ours. In ch. 7 the information that was reserved for us concerned Ezra's skill and devotion: it privileged us and created bonds of esteem with him. Contrasted to it in ch. 9 was his early silence in the presence of the impure community.

This controlled pattern of disclosure and reticence makes a link in the relations between the men Ezra and Nehemiah. These lie close to the center of the book's interest despite the silence of each about the other. We alone know his real reason for wanting to go to Jerusalem and who his informant was. Our degree of knowledge places us on the common ground between them and predisposes us to extend to Nehemiah the admiration we have for Ezra. On the other hand Nehemiah's three-day silence in Jerusalem implies an insufficiency among its inhabitants even after their purification from foreigners. The lack is unlikely to be remedied by the city walls whose logistical purpose is not plain, as we have seen. By implication the book looks ahead to a final communication and fulfillment, which will be the reading of the Law.

The autobiographical genre in the rest of Nehemiah 1–2 may have been a post-Exilic innovation.[4] Ezra also used it at times in Ezra 7–9, but unlike him Nehemiah is not introduced by any praise from the narrator. We do not know who this man is who mourns at the news from Jerusalem. The opening of the chapter recalls the introduction to some of the prophets: "The words of Nehemiah the son of Hacaliah."

---

[3] About the extent of the Memoirs scholars disagree on certain verses, especially those not in the first person and those that do not report Nehemiah's own activity. See especially D. J. A. Clines, "The Nehemiah Memoir: The Perils of Autobiography," in *What Does Eve Do To Help? And Other Readerly Questions to the Old Testament* (Sheffield: JSOT Press, 1990) 124–64.

[4] Shemaryahu Talmon, "Ezra and Nehemiah," *The Literary Guide to the Bible*, eds. Robert Alter and Frank Kermode (Cambridge, Mass.: Harvard University Press, 1987) 361.

(Compare Jer 1:1; Mic 1:1; Amos 1:1.) But he receives no call from YHWH and no prophetic word.

Form-critically we saw that much of Ezra's discourse is unique. As in the intercessions of Ezra and Moses in Deuteronomy, Nehemiah identifies himself and his family with the Jews. But it is not a public "sermon prayer" like Ezra's in Ezra 9–10, overheard by the "God-fearers of Israel." Nehemiah's prayer conforms to the biblical genre of the lamentations of the people, where the one praying is making supplication for the salvation of the community too.

Broadly, a prayer in this genre starts with an invocation of God; then follow a confession of sins, a request to YHWH to remember his people, and a plea for success. Nehemiah's own prayer is comprised of an expanded address formula to YHWH (v. 5), an appeal for a hearing (v. 6a),[5] a confession in his own name and that of his family and the people (vv. 6b-7), and an appeal to YHWH's promises (vv. 8-9), followed by a supplication for the people (v. 10) and for his personal situation (v. 11a). While none of these elements is unfamiliar except the last one, their combination in this way is without parallel in Scripture.

The convention makes the anomalies all the more striking. He does not say what the sins were or that the people will no longer commit them. He speaks of the conditional covenant but asks YHWH's help despite the people's corruption. He alludes to sins condemned already by Moses, the punishment for which had been the Exile.[6]

The prayer is a composition to suit the current situation by someone conversant with the tradition but not bound to it.[7] The emphasis on prayer in Nehemiah 1 and 2:1-10 shows that royal permission is once more to be seen as the instrument of divine initiative.

Rhetorical Audience

In Ezra 9–10 Ezra so coordinated his prayer and his audiences that the people's response to the exogamy crisis answered his petitions to YHWH. Nehemiah prays alone in Persia, far away from the Jerusalemites whose cooperation he wants to win. Moreover, his behavior is blatantly at odds with the situation at hand. He makes no particular attempt to persuade them that the works will alleviate their distress. He does not say who the enemy is that threatens the city. For three days

---

[5] Compare 1 Kings 8:28-29; 2 Chron 6:40; 7:15; Ps 130:2; Isa 37:17.

[6] Antonius H. J. Gunneweg, *Nehemia*. KAT 19/2 (Gütersloh : Gerd Mohn, 1987) 49.

[7] H. G. M. Williamson, *Ezra, Nehemiah* (Waco, Texas: Word Books, 1985) 167.

he says nothing at all to the people or his officers, and gives no hint of his opinions (Neh 2:11). He finally makes a speech, but he does not record it. In any case the people pitch in snappily, apparently without much need of persuasion: "And I told them [of] the hand of my God which was good upon me, and also [of] the words of the king which he had spoken to me. And they said, 'Let us rise up and build.' So they strengthened their hands for the good." (2:18) Similarly, no grounds are supplied for the opposition of Sanballat and Tobiah.

In Ezra 9–10 Ezra had kept silence too, but in order to heighten the impact of his mourning gestures and his words. He later withdrew from public sight so that the people themselves might take the initiative for the purification of their families. On the other hand, the public reticence of Nehemiah is not matched by any public discourse, and the people are not called to take responsibility for the project.

The absence of witnesses to Nehemiah's prayer and YHWH's continuing silence bring out the role of the current listener. We alone overhear his solitary prayer to YHWH. He tells the people that they "see" the trouble (2:17). Actually we are the only ones who receive a description of his solitary ride. Earlier he had not "told" them his plans. Now he simply "tells" them of his divine favor and the king's message in words that we do not need to hear. Neither had we heard the king give his permission (2:6, 8). If he or the people of the day were the most important rhetorical audiences these words might have been reported. As it is the people quickly respond: "Let us rise up and build!"—a verbal phrase that only we know Nehemiah repeats to the enemies later (2:17-18, 20). His prayer and petition are addressed to YHWH and the king respectively, but separately. On a deeper level they are meant for us, their only common audience. We in our time and place are the privileged audience, the only ones who can both be moved by his prayer and instructed by all his actions.

The memoir genre itself brings the realities of Persian Judah forward to us by being a first-hand written interpretation available to anyone. We are now invited to engage in the covenant and to judge our response in light of the exiles in Ezra 9–10. In those chapters, there was no avoiding the hard questions. Now, regarding the enemies and the foreign families, we are asked if we stand with the "God-fearers" or not. Nehemiah 1–2 is reaching out across time to all the listeners to the Memoirs, contemporary and future. We are drawn into the network of ties among leadership, community, tradition, belief, and action. Do we agree that the hand of God is on Nehemiah although only he says so? Is the Restoration YHWH's work? What is our place in their world, and theirs in ours?

Rhetorical Strategy

The Book of Nehemiah is continuing the theological question of how to act in the world. The Torah that is the heart's delight of Ezra is a form-giving force. It teaches the faithful how to perform acts—social, common and sacrificial—in a way that sanctifies the world. Now that the Judahites have made a preliminary step in bringing their families within the Torah, the rhetorical strategy here is to extend that system and invite us in.

In Nehemiah's prayer to Yhwh and his brief exchanges with the king and the people the species of rhetoric is therefore deliberative in regard to them and epideictic in regard to us. He seeks to persuade Yhwh, the king, and the people to respectively grant his prayer, give him leave, and do his bidding. These actions are in the present-day of the chapter, but he also wants us to hold his point of view in our present. For us the rhetoric is not deliberative: we are in no position to resolve the Judahites' crises; nor is it juridical, because Nehemiah, like Ezra, freely admits the guilt of his family and people. Epideictic rhetoric seeks the deepening of values such as the honorable and the good, or belief and faith. We, the listeners to the Memoirs, are first among the intended agents of this change in attitude.

Pathos is the principal mode of persuasion here. In Ezra 4 and partially in chs. 7 and 9–10 the rhetoric used the mode of argumentation called "logos" or the proof, actual or apparent, provided by the content of the speeches and documents. That is, the enemies in Ezra 4 sought to prove their points to the kings by presenting matters from their own perspective and they were undermined by a counter-version in 5–6. In Ezra 1, 7, 9–10, and somewhat in 4 the argument relied on "ethos" or the persuasive qualities of one's character or stature. Here, by contrast, we learn directly about Nehemiah's mission but not about his qualities. The narrator does not apply an epithet to him as with Ezra, "the scribe skilled in the law of Moses," to whom the king gave—"according to the hand of Yhwh his God upon him—all he requested" (Ezra 7:6). Nor do we know that Yhwh has roused his spirit like that of Cyrus (Ezra 1:1). Indeed, only at the end of his prayer does he even state his position in the court (Neh 1:11).

The king makes Nehemiah his emissary with warrants of requisition for matériel. But Nehemiah does not use performative language, the kind that creates realities by its very utterance like the edicts of the kings earlier. He gives the king's letters to the governors of the province without recorded comment, and he says nothing to the people at first until he uses the first person plural in the hortative: "Let us rise up and build" (Neh 2:18).

Instead, the rhetoric here uses "pathos," the appeal to the emotions and the most universal mode of persuasion. We were already meant to be stirred by Ezra's dramatic gestures of shock and anguish when he learned the news of the intermarriages in Ezra 9–10. They amplified his ethical appeal. Here the pitch to our feelings is all the keener since the argument rests squarely on it rather than on the person of Nehemiah or the logic of his remarks.

Rhetorical Devices

Nehemiah therefore does not speak in a way that breaks down into enthymemes. His purpose is not to propose the repair work systematically but to use the people's sorry state as the *topos* or topic through which to promote the deeper issue—our own engagement in the faith that should ground the identity of the Judahites. Rhetorically the walls are raised but not closed: they embrace the Judahites but invite us in too.

Nehemiah uses many of the patterns suitable to discourse of the species pathos.[8] They color the emotions of the audience, who should begin to feel that the speaker is right. The two major techniques are concrete speech and the projection of the desired emotions by the communicator.[9] Such a speaker sharpens the oral picture by lively description and other means that make the issue fully present to the listeners. Examples, repetition, accentuation, and the amplification of ideas make for spirited emotional discourse.

Nehemiah's prayer is not intended to be logical. He professes his faith that the people's disobedience leads to Exile and obedience to a homecoming, but the point is hardly a rational proposition since the people are already back from Persia. Rather, the diaspora and return are presented as examples of YHWH's justice. Argument by example is a mark of pathos. Justice will, he trusts, be done again.

The role of authority is always very important in any rhetoric touching the passions.[10] Hence when he does address the people Nehemiah's few words are about the hand of YHWH upon him and the mandate of the king.

Men suddenly arrive with stories of misery in Jerusalem; Nehemiah fasts pitiably for four long months and prays concerning the

[8] *Pathopeia* is a general term for the arousal of passion and emotion.

[9] Timothy A. Lenchak, *"Choose Life!" A Rhetorical-Critical Investigation of Deuteronomy 28,69–30,20* (Rome: Pontifical Biblical Institute, 1993) 129.

[10] Georges Molinié, *Dictionnaire de rhétorique*. Les Usuels de poche 8074, eds. Mireille Huchon and Michel Simonin (Paris: Librairie générale française, 1992) 265.

unnamed "man" (1:11); tension is high in the royal banquet hall; Nehemiah is silent, then stirs the people to action; the clash with his enemies ends in suspense—these scenes evoke excitement and sympathy in us. The first episodes in Susa are especially strong in their dramatic appeal. Ezra had sat disconsolate for several hours; Nehemiah goes one better and mourns for days on end. Months later, in a moment of ease when the king has his wine before him and his consort beside him, Nehemiah dares to speak of his anguish. He makes the tart retort: "Why should my face not be sad, when the city, the place (lit. "house") of my fathers' sepulchres, lies waste, and its gates have been destroyed (lit. "eaten") by fire?" (Neh 2:3). At first he does not mention Jerusalem or its walls lest the king remember that the Judahites' enemies had once called it rebellious and wicked ("If this city is rebuilt and its walls finished, you will then have no tax revenue . . ." [Ezra 4:12, 16]). He says instead that he wants to honor his ancestors' graves. Who could resist such an emotional appeal?

The suspense heightens when the king counters with a question of his own: "'For what do you make request?' So [Nehemiah] prayed to the God of the heavens." The king is a daunting figure even in the act of granting the request. He complies by asking still more questions: "How long will your journey last, and when will you return?" (2:6). Nehemiah dares to press him for *laissez-passer* and requisition notices. Now he mentions the wall (2:8). But still he obtains all that he needs.

We knew immediately that Ezra would succeed because he was favored by Yhwh (Ezra 7:6). It is only as the suspense of this scene winds down that we know the same of Nehemiah: "the good hand of [his] God was upon [him]" (2:8).

The vivid and, for Ezra–Nehemiah, protracted description of the night ride around the ruined city is another a device of pathetic discourse.[11] The dramatic length of that "crossing" (2:7) contrasts with the curt description of the "crossing" (2:14) from Persia: "Then I came to the governors of the province Beyond the River. . . . So I came to Jerusalem . . ." (Neh 2:9, 11).

Vocabulary

Most of all it is the vocabulary that carries the emotional tone. According to rhetorical theory pathos can be reinforced by the repeated use of emphatic diction such as second-person pronouns, words from

[11] Such vivid description is called *demonstratio.* "Apostrophe" is the term for amplication of detail.

national or ethnic history evoking bonding and pride or disgust, and words of emotion like "good," "evil," "war," and "death."[12] All these types are present in Nehemiah 1–2.

The diction makes ample use of the metaphoric and concrete possibilities of Hebrew. YHWH is imagined with "ears" and "eyes" (1:6, 11). The exiles are scattered at the farthest horizon (lit. "edge of the skies," or "heavens") (1:9). Nehemiah's "face" and "heart" are sad (lit. "evil") (2:2, 3). In private he ominously calls the king "this man" (1:11).

Many phrases are all the more gripping in that they are unique in Hebrew Scripture: the Judahites are "in great trouble (lit. "evil") and shame" (1:3); Nehemiah confesses "the sins (plural) of the sons of Israel" (1:6); "the place (lit. "house") of [one's] fathers' sepulchres" must be repaired (2:3).

Like Ezra's prayer, Nehemiah's conveys his solidarity with the Israelites by switching into the first person plural : ". . . hear the prayer of your slave . . . on [behalf of] the sons of Israel your slaves, confessing the sins of the sons of Israel, which we have sinned against you" (Neh 1:7).

Other repetitions raise the tension.[13] YHWH "keeps" covenant with those who "keep" the Law (1:5), but this people has not "kept" the commandments that YHWH "commanded [his] slave Moses." Will YHWH remember the word that he "commanded [his] slave Moses" now (1:7-8)? We want YHWH to "hear" the prayer (1:6); we are worried when the enemy Sanballat "hears" of the plan (2:10). Nehemiah "hears" that Jerusalem is in "evil" or trouble, and he describes the people's plight to them as "evil" (1:3-4; 2:17) after praying that YHWH "hear" him (1:6). He stirs the people with an appeal to their honor: "Come (lit. "go"), let us build the wall of Jerusalem, that we may no longer suffer (lit. "be") disgrace" (2:17). Then, dramatically, the hostile trio "hear" of the plan and it is "evil" or unpleasant for them (2:10).

Two polar terms expressive of emotion and value are particularly frequent. "Evil" occurs six times and "good" eight times.[14] "Evil" is among Nehemiah's first words to the people, in 2:17, and the name of one of Nehemiah's opponents, Tobiah, puns on the Hebrew for "good" (2:19).

"Slave" is used twelve times in nine verses in Nehemiah 1–2. The Judahites and Nehemiah are "slaves" in relation, like Moses (1:7, 8), to YHWH or to the king. The frequency could be in compensation for the loss of kingship, underscoring the equality between the leader and the

---

[12] Lenchak, *Life* 142.

[13] The rhetorical technique of repetition is called *epanalepsis*.

[14] "Evil": 1:3; 2:1, 2 [2x], 3, 10, and "good": 2:5 [2x], 6, 7, 8, 10, 18 [2x].

people—servants all before the Law of Moses, servant of God. It is a denigrating contrast that Tobiah is "slave" to Sanballat.

Part of these chapters' significance is in the links and distinctions between Ezra and Nehemiah. First, note these differences:

- Ezra's genealogy is one of the longest in Scripture; Nehemiah has none.
- Ezra has ascendancy over the king according to the law of YHWH (Ezra 7:6); Nehemiah is afraid of the king (Neh 2:2).
- Ezra refuses to ask for a guard (Ezra 8:22); Nehemiah is assigned one (Neh 2:9).
- Ezra travels with volunteers who are fellow Jews described genealogically (Ezra 8:1-29); Nehemiah travels with an assigned anonymous entourage.
- Ezra's departure echoes the Exodus experience of liberation; Nehemiah has given a return date (2:6).
- In Jerusalem Ezra sits immobile but in public before speaking persuasively; Nehemiah makes a night journey alone, informing no one.
- In stages Ezra convinces the Judahites by skillful language arts; after Nehemiah makes a single statement the people rush to start work. He then repeats their words, "arise" and "build" (Neh 2:17-20).
- Ezra is a priest and scribe, Nehemiah a layman.

Despite these differences the men's manner and projects bear similarities, as mentioned in the Introduction to this chapter. The vocabulary further directs our attention to their relationship. Ezra "mourned" in Ezra 10:6, with the same verb as Nehemiah here in Neh 1:4. Ezra also calls himself a "slave" of YHWH in relation to the king and his construction project, described as a wall or "fence": "For we are slaves; but in our slavery our God did not abandon us but has . . . [given] us a fence in Judah and in Jerusalem" (Ezra 9:9).[15] Ezra had set his heart to study the Law of YHWH, to do and teach it (Ezra 7:10). YHWH has put plans for Jerusalem into Nehemiah's heart (Neh 2:12) as he did with the king's heart to agree to Ezra's plan (Ezra 7:27). The people had the heart to follow Nehemiah's plan (Neh 4:6 [MT 3:38]). In all of the Old Testament "the good hand of God" is only on Ezra, the people under him, and Nehemiah (Ezra 7:9; 8:18; Neh 2:8). The Hebrew words for "betray" and "people" are used in Ezra 10:2 and Neh 1:8, two of only

---

[15] Also the elders in Ezra 5:11: "We are the slaves of the God of heaven and earth and we are building the house which was built many years ago which a great king of Israel built and finished."

five occurrences together in Scripture. "And Shecaniah . . . replied to Ezra, saying, 'We have betrayed our God and married (lit. "made to dwell") foreign women from the peoples of the land but now there is hope for Israel concerning this.'" Compare Nehemiah quoting YHWH here: "'If you are unfaithful (or: betraying), I will scatter you among the peoples; but if you return to me and keep my commandments and do them, though your dispersed [people] are at the farthest horizon, I will gather them from there . . . '" (Neh 1:8-9). "Escaped remnant" is a phrase used in the book only by Ezra and Nehemiah.[16] As for the escort of "army officers (or: chiefs) and horsemen," Nehemiah is granted what Ezra declines to ask for in the same words (Neh 2:9; Ezra 8:22).

The most telling similarity is in their joint relation to Moses' rhetoric. In Ezra 9–10 Ezra had alluded freely but pointedly to Deuteronomy 7 and its warnings against exogamy. Now Nehemiah builds on the same discourse of Moses: ". . . the LORD (lit. "YHWH") loves you, and is keeping the oath which he swore to your fathers, that the LORD (lit. "YHWH") has brought you out with a mighty hand, and redeemed you from the house of bondage, from the hand of Pharaoh king of Egypt. . . . Know therefore that the LORD (lit. "YHWH") your God is God, the faithful God who maintains (lit. "keeps") covenant loyalty (lit. "covenant and lovingkindness") with those who love him and keep his commandments, to a thousand generations" (Deut 7:9; also 5:10). Compare Nehemiah: "Please, YHWH, God of the heavens, the great and fearsome God who keeps covenant and lovingkindness with those who love him and keep his commandments. . . . They are your slaves and your people, whom you have redeemed by your great power and by your strong hand" (Neh 1:5, 10).

Nehemiah locates himself among those thousand generations. He uses the same word "redeem" with its implications of the Exodus,[17] and he invokes the commandments, statutes, ordinances, and words commanded to Moses (Neh 1:7-8). Exceptionally for him, he uses "YHWH" here, the divine name revealed to Moses.[18] The title "great and fearsome God" is uniquely used by Moses, Nehemiah, and Daniel.[19]

---

[16] "Escaped remnant": *pᵉlêṭāh* in Ezra 9:8, 13, 14, 15; Neh 1:2. Also "survivors" and "remain" as nifal variants of *šaʾar* are used only by Ezra (Ezra 9:15), Nehemiah (Neh 1:2), and Cyrus (Ezra 1:4) and Hanani (Neh 1:3), their interlocutors in the matter of the crises.

[17] F. Charles Fensham, *The Books of Ezra and Nehemiah* (Grand Rapids: Eerdmans, 1982) 156.

[18] And in Neh 5:13; elsewhere *ʾElohîm*. The Ezra Memoirs use both titles.

[19] Deut 7:21; 10:17; Dan 9:4; Neh 1:5, with *ʾEl* or *ʾElohîm*. The worshipers in Neh 9:32 speak of "our God, the great and mighty and awesome God." Neh 4:14 (MT 4:8): "YHWH [who is] great and fearsome."

Nehemiah 1 begins: "The words of Nehemiah." Deuteronomy begins: "These words which Moses spoke to all Israel beyond the Jordan." Moses had gone on in Deuteronomy 7, "And he will hand their kings over to you" (v. 24). Is this one reason why Nehemiah now has easy sway over the king of Persia?

The larger frame of Deuteronomy 7 is the covenanted election of Israel in contrast to the peoples of the land (7:1-8). Nehemiah's rhetorical reliance on it shows that his wall-building is not just a security measure, nor is his prayer simply a plea for help against the king's anger. The full shape of the issue is made plainer when one realizes that Nehemiah's prayer also echoes Deuteronomy 29–30. This is the last discourse of Moses, spoken to the assembly, telling them they are becoming a people. YHWH is making a covenant with them and indeed with those who are not there that day (Deut 29:11-14 [MT 29:12-15]).

Here Moses again recalls the Exodus and the covenant given for generations to come. He foresees exile and diaspora, trials to be ended by the people's return to obedience: "Even if you are exiled to the ends of the world (lit. "the heavens"), from there the LORD (lit. "YHWH") your God will gather you, and from there he will bring you back" (Deut 30:4). Nehemiah 1:8-9 is largely a paraphrase of these promises in Deut 30:1-5.

Nehemiah's prayer closed with a petition for "success" and "mercy." At the end of his exchange with his enemies he was confident that YHWH would make the Judahites "successful." Here are the comparable words in the assurances of Moses' speech: "Therefore diligently observe the words of this covenant, in order that you may succeed in everything you do. . . . [H]e will make you more prosperous (lit. "good") and numerous than your ancestors (lit. "fathers") . . . and the LORD (lit. "YHWH") will make you abundantly prosperous (lit. "for the good") in all your undertakings (lit. "the deeds of your hand")" (Deut 29:9 [MT 29:8]; 30:5, 9).

Nehemiah says nothing of Ezra at all. It is the vocabulary more than the plot that does the job of putting them together. Ezra and Nehemiah relate to one another generally through the repeated patterns of the episodes: return, obstacle, project, success, and celebration. We further suggested that in this new post-Exilic world the rebuilding of the walls with Nehemiah fills a role like that of the settlement of the land after the Sinai experience of commitment with Ezra. But more specifically the words of Moses are their *lingua franca*.

For example, many of the words common to the language of Ezra and Nehemiah also punctuate this discourse of Moses. We have already seen how the Hebrew for "heart" is prominent in the rhetorical landscape surrounding Nehemiah, Ezra, the kings of Persia, and the people.[20] It is also a leitmotif of Deuteronomy and chs. 29–30 contain twelve of its fifty-one appearances there, after which the word vanishes from that book. The expression "for [the] good" already linked Ezra and Moses; now it does the same for Nehemiah.[21] Ezra, Nehemiah, and Moses are verbally associated.

In many ways neither Ezra nor Nehemiah is anything like Moses. Neither has a birth story, call experience, or theophany. Nehemiah's weapon is not a magic staff but a dossier of official documents. He is a courtier to a foreign king as Moses was, but Nehemiah will return to Persia. He is a royal delegate, not a rebel, as only his enemies could suggest (Neh 2:19). He does not lead the people out but rather walls them in. There is no question for him of ownership of the Land or circumcision. Nehemiah does speak to God on behalf of the people as Moses had done, but the deuteronomic passage he most directly borrows from is a direct address by Moses to the people, and we have seen that Nehemiah speaks hardly two sentences to them.

Nevertheless Deuteronomy 29–30 records Moses' words before he appoints his successor. The similarities and pointed differences between those chapters and these raise the possibility that Nehemiah is a new and different kind of Moses, fulfilling the role in his society that Moses had in his.

In this he matches Ezra, who was presented in Ezra 7 as a successor to Moses—a "scribe skilled in [his] law," in whose "hand" it is. Nehemiah is a double counterfoil to Moses, less like him than Ezra yet living some elements of his life and speaking his words.

Leadership in the new Israel is thus rooted in the past but also circumscribed by it. The tradition has been claimed but divided between two very different men, neither of whom fully resembles the model. The two men's prayers share between them the right to evoke the divine promises. The tradition is kept alive in an interpreted form such that it can never be abused as the prerogative of one religious party against another. No future ruler will be able to step forward as the only "Moses redux."

Next, all the commentaries register the parallels between Nehemiah 1–2 and Solomon's speech at the dedication of the Temple in 1 Kings 8 and 2 Chronicles 6. Nehemiah lays claim to its promise that YHWH would hear a sincere supplicant in a foreign land.[22] Nehemiah's address to YHWH as the God of the heavens who "keeps covenant and lovingkindness" (Neh 1:5) compares to 1 Kings 8:23 (and 2 Chron 6:14-

---

[20] Ezra 7:10, 27; Neh 2:10; 4:6 [MT 3:38].

[21] Ezra 9:12; Deut 23:7 and Neh 2:18; Deut 28:11; 30:9.

[22] 1 Kings 8:46-51; 2 Chron 6:36-39.

15): "O LORD (lit. "YHWH"), God of Israel, there is no God like you, in heaven above or on earth beneath, keeping covenant and showing steadfast love (or: lovingkindness) for your servants (or: slaves) who walk before you with all their heart." And "the place which I have chosen to make my name inhabit there" (Neh 1:9) fits beside 1 Kings 8:29 (and 2 Chron 6:20): "this house, the place of which you said, 'My name shall be there,' that you may heed the prayer that your servant (or: slave) prays toward this place . . . ."

Solomon and Nehemiah pray that YHWH's ear be attentive and his eyes watchful.[23] Solomon's petition concerns the Temple, which is not enough to contain YHWH (v. 18). That is, YHWH is also approachable beyond the Temple, in places like Susa where Nehemiah prays. Nehemiah calls his supplication "the prayer of your slave" or "of your slaves," that is, YHWH's. The expression occurs only in the speech of Solomon, Nehemiah, and Daniel.[24]

Again at issue are the plans and hopes in the "heart" of an Israelite: "whatever prayer, whatever plea there is from any individual or from all your people Israel, all knowing the afflictions of their own hearts so that they stretch out their own hands toward this house; then hear in heaven your dwelling place, forgive, act, and render to all whose hearts you know—according to all their ways, for only you know what is in every human heart" (1 Kings 8:38-39). See also 1 Kings 8:17-18 and its parallel 2 Chron 6:7 where Solomon says that his father David had wanted in his heart to build the Temple but was forbidden by YHWH.

It is one of the redactional oddities of the book that Nehemiah ignores the altar and Temple whose repair had so preoccupied Jeshua, Zerubbabel, and Sheshbazzar. These many allusions to Solomon's consecration of the first Temple go some way to bridging that gap, but the cross-reference to Israel's king means more.

It would be too simplistic a summary of the book to place a "practical, theocratic" school over against an "eschatological, visionary" school. The differences and similarities between Ezra and Nehemiah, and between the two of them and Moses and Solomon are a complex statement about leadership and heritage in post-Exilic Israel. The two men so allude to past leaders that their words revalidate tradition, but each in his own fashion. Ezra gives way to Nehemiah as Zerubbabel and Jeshua did to Sheshbazzar, who disappears in his turn. After the fall of the Davidic dynasty Israel's destiny will not again depend on one style of leadership or one ruling family. Israel's disastrous political history is not denied, but it is further repositioned in the alignment of

[23] 1 Kings 8:28-29; Neh 1:6, 11.
[24] 1 Kings 8:28; Dan 9:17; Neh 1:6, 11; 2 Chron 6:19.

values that marks the post-Exilic Restoration. The true scope of leadership is set out, just as the silence of Ezra in chs. 9–10 showed the relativity of oral persuasion. Again the implied antithesis is the enduring
sovereignty of YHWH.

The heart, the mind, and the will: Nehemiah's epideictic and deliberative argument by "pathos" balances Ezra's deliberative argument
by "logos" and "ethos" in Ezra 7. The variety of rhetoric demonstrates
the importance of adhering to the Law fully. As was said in Deuteronomy, from which both men quote: "You shall love the LORD your God
with all your heart, and with all your soul, and with all your might"
(Deut 6:5).

Conclusion

As much as the stone walls, what is thrown around Jerusalem is
living tradition, a rampart from which to survey the past and the future. The Temple is already rebuilt because the community cannot
change without liturgy, the link to the past that keeps memory—and
tradition—alive. That tradition, out of which Ezra and Nehemiah
speak, is now reinforced as the compass of the people's identity, but in
ways whose variation invites us in as well, we who come after them
and whose circumstances are different again. If tradition is to be a
source for reform new generations must always be at home in it, as
Ezra and Nehemiah are in the language of Moses and Solomon. For
two such different characters to speak through the tradition in the
modes of both ethos and pathos shows the adaptability of interpreted
tradition as a hermeneutic of changing realities.

Glenn Loury, an African American leader, has applied a reading of
Nehemiah 1–2 to his people. "What does it really *mean* for a city not to
have walls?" he asks. "It's a powerful metaphor, and closely related to
black people's situation today. A city without walls has no integrity, or
structure; it is subject to the vagaries of any fad or fancy. Without walls,
you are lost, as opposed to having some kind of internally derived
sense of who you are to help you decide what you will and won't do."[25]

Ezra's rhetorical strategies insisted that Israel's identity flows from
its recollection and celebration of the covenant. Now Nehemiah adds
that Israel must also transmit it. Covenant membership and endoga-
mous purity are tools of identity, not absolute barriers. It is true that
the people of the land could not participate in the work of Ezra 4. On
the other hand, the speech in Nehemiah 1–2 is closely directed to those

[25] Robert S. Boynton, "Loury's Exodus," *The New Yorker* May 1, 1995, 41.

who listen to it after the events themselves. Jerusalem is physically closed but rhetorically opened by the reconstruction of its walls. Israel is helped in a new way to find its claim to meaning between the fact of historical transcience and the enduring hope of divine redemption.

This strategy demonstrates again the permeability of time in Ezra–Nehemiah. In Ezra 4–5 the account of the past was reshaped theologically. In Ezra 7 Ezra's plans in the present were described and realized through the eternal perspective of Yhwh's will. Now, by privileging the listeners to the book with knowledge beyond that of the characters, Nehemiah 1–2 brings us and our time, the book's future, directly within the ambit of Israel's Restoration. Gaps in time are breached like the holes in the wall.

The function of a wall, and its role in the world of symbols, is to defend from without and embrace from within.[26] It is no wonder that the rabbis chose the wall or fence as a symbol of the rabbinic law defending the Torah.[27] Here the Torah that will be proclaimed is surrounded by a "wall" of tradition, but with gates that open to the past and the future. It is we too, after Nehemiah's time, who are asked to "remember the word which [Yhwh] commanded [his] slave Moses" long ago and to "remember Yhwh" (1:8; 4:14).

That is why Nehemiah dismisses the enemies with the curse of being forgotten: "[T]o you there will be no portion or right or memorial in Jerusalem" (Neh 2:20). Not to remember or be remembered is to be cast outside this redeeming synthesis of time. "They refused to obey, and did not remember the wonders which you performed among them." Yhwh is to remember Nehemiah for his good and the enemies for their evil (Neh 9:17 and 5:19; 6:14; 13:14, 22, 29, 31).

Like Ezra, Nehemiah is not a character of much psychological depth or verisimilitude. His speech too has full meaning only in relation to that of others, here Moses and Solomon. He does not speak of the Temple, the Law, or the prophets by name. Neither is the real issue the range of Jerusalem's geographical boundaries or its degree of holiness. Rather his words apply concretely and extend temporally the book's theology of history and national self-definition.

The patterns in the plot and the differences and similarities between the men, and between each of them and Moses, testify to a whole Torah tradition, presented variously to show its inherent diversity. No single reading of the Mosaic heritage can be the only truth since here Scripture itself tells different midrashes of it. Ezra–Nehemiah

---

[26] Juan Eduardo Cirlot, *A Dictionary of Symbols*, trans. Jack Sage (London: Routledge & Kegan Paul, 1962) 343.

[27] *m.ᵓAbot* 1:1.

is not as conformist as the actions of expulsion and walling-in make it seem, for in its dimension of language it is variant with itself. We are closer now to the climax of the reading of the Law in Nehemiah 9, but the rhetoric continues to contextualize it, and prevents one interpretation from shutting out others. The result is characteristic of Judaism even now: consensus in diversity across time through identity and praxis. As the Talmud says, the Word of God is like fire or a hammer breaking rock, dividing into many flames or fragments.[28]

---

[28] *b.Šabb.* 88b.

Chapter Seven
NEHEMIAH 3–7

Nehemiah's Memoir continues with five episodic chapters whose rhetorical exchanges are no less important for being brief. Immediately after Nehemiah tells his opponents that they will have no memorial in Jerusalem, a list is given of those who *are* remembered, the volunteer builders.[1] It includes the names of the people's fathers, but also their station and task in the restoration work. They are recorded not just for who they are but also for what they do. Nehemiah's name is not among them, although the High Priest's is, and nothing is said about the administrative tasks of his that must have been behind the work. Some commentators have concluded that it is élitism on his part not to participate in the physical labor, but in light of the persuasive language he uses it rather stresses that the people are interlocutors whose consent and participation are an indispensable part of the language strategies. The people's bustling energy here is the full answer to Nehemiah's prayer in 1:1 in which he had called them "[YHWH's] slaves who delight (or: want) to fear [his] name." Twice in the first line of ch. 3 Nehemiah writes that the site was consecrated.

The short arguments are not as full as elsewhere, but again the pattern is that an initiative by the Jews triggers opposition when discovered by the enemies.[2] Despite the thud of masons' hammers in the chapters, language is still the engine that brings changes. First Sanballat hears news and reacts with questions. He asks five questions in the presence of his associates and the army of Samaria. The Hebrew is puzzling, but the NRSV translation is as good as any: "What are these feeble Jews doing? Will they restore things? Will they sacrifice? Will they finish it in a day? Will they revive the stones out of the heaps of rubbish—and burned ones at that?" (Neh 4:2 [MT 3:34]). To the degree

---

[1] Some scholars dispute that the list of volunteer builders is part of the Nehemiah Memoir. The point is immaterial to our concern with the rhetoric.

[2] Note the similarities in language in Neh 2:10, 19; 4:1; 4:7; 6:1 (English).

that the original text is intelligible his questions seem to be a mixture of the straightforward interrogative ("What are [they] doing?"), the hyperbolic ("Will they finish in a day [or perhaps: today]?") and the metaphorical ("Will they revive the stones . . . ?"). His questions go unanswered. Instead, Tobiah makes a sarcastic statement of his own: "That stone wall they are building—any fox going up on it would break it down!"

While the Jews are active, restoring their city and their life, Sanballat has scarcely changed even his words. Already in Neh 2:19 when he first heard of Nehemiah's plan he had "mocked" them and asked what they were "doing": the same Hebrew verbs are used there and here (Neh 4:1-2). Sanballat's question about reviving the stones for the wall is an echo of Ezra's prayer for a revival of the people and a fence for protection in Ezra 9:8, 9, using the same Hebrew root for "revive."

Most disarming of all for the evildoers, they are quoted to us by Nehemiah, their opponent, who controls the tranmission of their words and can censor them altogether. He does so in 4:8 (MT 4:2) when they make undescribed plans: "and all plotted together to come and fight against Jerusalem and to cause confusion in it." What follows is not evident. Either the enemies plan to attack but the danger is reported each time, or they want disruptive stories to leak, in which case they also fail because the works continue nonetheless. In the meantime, in their quoted speech throughout Nehemiah 3–4, Sanballat and Tobiah are not in real dialogue with one another. They only make exclamations and air insults.

The enemies are deprived of the power of language and undone by the words of others. Nehemiah tells YHWH that the Jews are "despised" by them, a word whose implication in Scripture is that those who hold a chosen one of YHWH in such contempt are themselves condemned to insignificance (4:4 [MT 3:36]).[3] The Hebrew word for their "taunt" here is the "shame" of the Jews in Neh 1:3 and 2:17. The adversaries want to sow "confusion," a word used elsewhere only in Isa 32:6 in the telling maxim: "The fool [utters] error concerning the LORD."

These reversals of language mean the enemies' insults do turn back on their own head, as Nehemiah prays should happen. He wants those who hold the Jews as objects of contempt to become themselves objects of plunder (a Hebrew pun: *bûzzāh/bîzzāh*). Let them be exiles, as the Jews themselves had been: "Give them over as plunder in a land of captivity" (4:4 [MT 3:36]). The Jews, on the contrary, put their "heart"

---

[3] Manfred Görg, "בזה bazah," *Theological Dictionary of the Old Testament*, eds. G. Johannes Botterweck and Helmer Ringgren (2nd rev. ed. Grand Rapids: Eerdmans, 1977, reprint 1988) 2:63.

in their work, as the king did with his favor to them, as Ezra did with the study of the Law and Nehemiah with his planning ("heart" in Ezra 6:22; 7:10; Neh 2:12).

The enemies' words are now empty of power and sense. Their reports will be called their own invention (6:8); they will invent false prophecy; their blessing turns to a curse on themselves (13:2); their children will speak only foreign tongues (13:23). This is the meaning rhetorically of Nehemiah's curse that they should have no "portion or right or memorial" (Neh 2:20). The Jews transform heaps of broken stone into defenses, but their enemies pile up words in vain.

Nehemiah now prays as he did when he first learned of the state of Jerusalem. Then his petition was in the genre of a lament. Now it is more strongly worded, an "imprecatory prayer" that curses his enemies (3:36-37 [MT 4:4-5]). In his first prayer Nehemiah had repeated the received theology that Yhwh "keeps covenant and lovingkindness with those who love him and keep his commandments" (Neh 1:5). Since obedience to Yhwh brings blessings, and the enemies wish the opposite of the good of the Israelites, they must be opposed to Yhwh and suffer by Israel's blessing. The insult is against Yhwh and so the prayer hands vindication over to him.[4] By their enmity the Jews' opponents bring disaster on themselves, just as their own words have become self-curses. Nehemiah's prayer is effective since Yhwh frustrates their plot (Neh 4:15). While his adversaries' words are losing consequence, his words are gaining. Their failures bear out the power of his cursing prayer and thus his godliness.

This prayer is his own version of Jeremiah's in Jer 18:23: "Yet you, O Lord (lit. "Yhwh"), know / all their plotting to kill me. / Do not forgive their iniquity, / do not blot out their sin from your sight. / Let them be tripped up before you; / deal with them while you are angry."

Elsewhere, too, Nehemiah can speak like a prophet. Some of the exhortations are in the genre of a prophetic oracle: "Do not be afraid of them. Remember the Lord . . . Our God will fight for us" (4:14, 20 [MT 4:8, 20]). In the manner of Isaiah and Jeremiah he upbraids the people on matters of justice to the poor, shaking out his robe to accent his words with a typical symbolic gesture (5:6-13). The first line of the Book of Nehemiah sounds like the beginning of a prophetic book: "The words of Nehemiah, son of Hacaliah." And some of his vocabulary is shared only with the prophets, like "confusion" (4:8 [MT 4] and Isa 32:6).

---

[4] F. Charles Fensham, *The Books of Ezra and Nehemiah* (Grand Rapids: Eerdmans, 1982) 181. As other examples of the genre, among the psalms of imprecation are Psalms 35, 58, 59, 69, 109, 137.

The Talmud calls Nehemiah a prophet.[5] Indeed, like a prophet he knows intuitively that God had not sent Shemaiah to him (6:12) and he acclaims with confidence that God put it into his mind to call the assembly (7:5). But no explicit mention is made of any prophet here, unlike in Ezra's prayer in Ezra 9:11, and in Ezra 5:1 and 6:14 where Haggai and Zechariah encourage the building project. Nehemiah employs language shared with prophets without being fully one himself. Specifically, he speaks like Moses, now in Moses' prophetic role.

We have seen how some of Ezra's speech and the description of his work were also in the idiom of prophecy. Prophetic discourse now becomes another of the ties between the two protagonists of Ezra–Nehemiah, and between both of them and Moses. In Ezra 6 the prophets were active in inspiring the people but in words we never heard. Ezra and now Nehemiah speak prophetic language, but without the full call and charism. Here those who are called prophets are false ones (Neh 6:12, 14). Ezra–Nehemiah is continuing the prophetic tradition in rhetorical ways that outstrip the movement itself. Again we see that one of the theological intentions of the book is to lay out new relations of faith to power and leadership.

Nehemiah's remarks after his prayer in these chapters are largely deliberative, statements made to do things and to get things done. As previously with the king and us as his audiences he uses "pathos," the appeal to the emotions, in rallying the Jews to fight for their families and homes (Neh 4:14 [MT 8]). They are not to "fear" the enemy, for YHWH is "great and fearsome"—the same two adjectives with Deuteronomic connections that he already used in his prayer in ch. 1. Similarly when the Israelites were defending their freedom in the Exodus, Moses told them not to "fear" the Egyptians but only "fear" YHWH (Exod 20:20). In their struggle now they must "remember" YHWH who Nehemiah had prayed would "remember" his own commands to Moses (1:8; 4:14 [MT 4:8]).

Nehemiah uses the language of "holy war" whose chief location is among Moses' words in Deuteronomy. Enemies conspire; the people call on YHWH for help; their resources are limited; they form battle lines according to tribal levy; they are urged not to fear; the enemy's plans are frustrated.[6] Deuteronomy 7:16-26 is in the genre of Holy War and Nehemiah 1–2, we saw, shares particular diction with that chapter.

Through the scan of all this verbal network Nehemiah continues to touch the tradition of Moses and Deuteronomy. This overlay ties to-

---

[5] *b.Ber.* 13a calls him a prophet in relation to Neh 9:7, attributed by the Babylonian Talmud to him, inspired by the "spirit."

[6] Joseph Blenkinsopp, *Ezra–Nehemiah* (Philadelphia: Westminster, 1988) 247.

gether his earlier discourse and these shorter interventions in chs. 3–7. It further vilifies his adversaries and gives authority to the orders and encouragement that form the greater part of his remarks here: "I stationed the people. . . . 'Rally to us. . . . Let every man and his servant pass the night in Jerusalem. . . .'" Most important, it shows again that the tradition is still available as a medium for expressing and shaping Israel's life without any leader expropriating the unique stature of Moses himself.

Next, ch. 5 describes a crisis in Judahite society that allows us to test this reading. The people complain that their rich countrymen are driving them into debt-slavery. To borrow money in Israel one needed a pledge—an article of clothing for a small loan, but for a larger loan one's property could be mortgaged. In extreme need the law allowed the mortgage of oneself or one's children whose labor would clear the debt.[7] The people here criticize not Nehemiah, but their wealthy Jewish brothers who hold their mortgages.

Reforms of such problems were not actually part of Nehemiah's imperial mission. He never deals with the root cause, which is land ownership, nor does he release the slaves. But justice is a divine ordinance. "Should you not walk in the fear of our God . . . ?" he asks. The issue is put to him and he intervenes. The matter becomes a test of his commitment to his words, like the issue of exogamy for Ezra.

In Ezra's prayer in ch. 9 the prophets, the "slaves" of YHWH, had given the Law to the people who were "slaves" to the Persians. Now, however, contrary to the Law the poor are being oppressed by being reduced to "slavery" unjustly.

Nehemiah calls an assembly of all the people and addresses them. His response draws on YHWH's words to Moses in Exodus 21, Moses' own revelation of the Law in Deuteronomy 15, as well as the Holiness Code in Leviticus 25. In these traditions debt slavery was allowed, but not to the point of making destitute the poorest citizens.[8]

Jeremiah 34:8-21 is an example of a similar complaint about impossible debt. The prophet receives a divine message much like Nehemiah's own speech here: "Therefore, thus says the LORD: You have not obeyed me by granting a release to your neighbors and friends . . . ." The brotherhood of the people is spoken of in a judgment sealed with a ritual curse. In Jeremiah the curse in the name of the God

---

[7] David J. A. Clines, *Ezra, Nehemiah, Esther* (Grand Rapids: Eerdmans, 1984) 165–67.

[8] Debt slavery is allowed in Exod 21:1-11; 22:24-26 (English 25-27); 23:11; Lev 25:47-54; Deut 15:12-18; 24:10-13. But it is illegal to repossess pledges in the case of the poor according to Exod 22:24 (English 25); Lev 25:36; Deut 24:10-11.

of the Exodus is symbolized by walking through animal halves. Here Nehemiah shakes out his garment. That is, YHWH will shake them out of their possessions if they disobey. In Nehemiah priests also receive the oath and the assembly replies heartily.

Again the cross-resemblances among Nehemiah's Memoirs and these Mosaic, legal, and Jeremiah texts reinforce his strategy of argumentation through adapted tradition. It is convincing, for on hearing him the people fall silent "and could not find a word to say" (5:8). The difference between Nehemiah's words and the legislation and prophecy is that he includes himself among the guilty. He foregoes the rights that are strictly his as a creditor. Further, in 5:14 he renounces the tax revenue for his own use that Persian custom allowed.[9]

The book is ambiguous about Nehemiah's legal and political prerogatives. The "cry" of the people (5:1) is a technical and legal term for a legal remedy. Here exceptionally it is made by women also. The king did not name him governor in ch. 2, but in 5:14 he speaks as though he were. (Who might have appointed him, however, is unclear in the Hebrew, which is incomplete.)

Nehemiah uses the same strategy as Ezra had: call a general assembly to isolate the opposition and put them on the spot. Take quick action. His first argument is nothing more than fiscal common sense. (Again the Hebrew is garbled.) Jews were supposed to redeem compatriots sold into debt slavery to foreigners. There seems to be a waste of money because new indebtedness keeps raising the expense of that obligation beyond the profit from the labor of the debt slaves in Jewish employ.

Next, in 5:9, he uses "pathos" and warns them of the "taunts" or shame that will be upon them if they do not honor God. The word here is the one that Nehemiah had already used to win the consent of the king and to stir the people to the building of the wall. He had begged YHWH to turn such shame on the heads of the enemies.[10] Now the Judahites risk having it fall back on them.

Nehemiah's words are greater than the man himself, he who had no genealogy or epithet in his introduction (Nehemiah 1). He calls on God to remember him (5:19), but the depth and character of his remarks are conveyed through the woven strands of Israelite heritage. Perhaps this is why the text prevaricates in 5:9 over the grammatical person of the speaker. He is quoting himself, but the consonantal Hebrew spells "he said." He is, as it were, asking YHWH to remember him

---

[9] Fensham, *Books of Ezra and Nehemiah* 197; Clines, *Ezra, Nehemiah, Esther* 170.
[10] Neh 1:3; 2:17; 4:4 (MT 3:26).

since he himself is remembering the tradition and is present to us through it. His enemies he cursed to obscurity in 2:20.

After the Return from Exile the prophets Haggai and Zechariah had proposed Zerubbabel and Jeshua as messianic figures, heralding a perfected order.[11] But nothing here would allow us to see the society as eschatologically perfect or Nehemiah as a Messiah-King. Indeed, it is the Judahites' enemies who put it about that he will be crowned. They threaten him with letters and rumors that he is attempting a coup against Persia. They press him to come and talk to them (6:7). Again communication and language are the stimulus to action.

The enemies think that the Judahites' "hands will drop" from the work (6:9)—an expression that the foes of Zerubbabel and Jeshua had already used in vain (Ezra 4:4). Nehemiah prays instead that God strengthen his hands, a prayer that is an inversion of the sense and the Hebrew word order of the enemies' words. Then the false prophet Shemaiah says that others are coming to kill Nehemiah when he himself is in fact a conspirator as recounted to us by the intended victim himself. Again language fails the enemies in the same degree as their plans.

In opposite ways YHWH is to "remember" Tobiah's animosity *(lᵉtôbîãh)* as he "remembers" Nehemiah "for [his] good" *(lᵉṭôbãh)* (5:19; 6:14). Of course reports from Tobiah's confederates about his "good deeds" *(ṭôbotâw)* do nothing to sway Nehemiah (6:19).

This series of episodes ends with only a passing mention that the wall is rebuilt (Neh 7:1). Of far greater length is another list of the repatriates' names. Nehemiah writes that YHWH inspired him to complete a census of the current population during which he found a genealogical register of the first repatriates (Neh 7:5). The previous list was in Ezra 2 and together they form an "inclusion" around the homecomings and the three building projects. Ezra 2 immediately leads to the building of the altar and to worship. Nehemiah 7 precedes the ceremony of reading the Torah. This envelope arrangement suggests a relation between altar-building and Torah-reading in which sacrifices and the Law complement one another as media of YHWH's sovereign presence. Nehemiah 7 brings the earlier group of exiles into the present and makes them participants in the celebration and dedication that follow immediately.[12]

The Books of Ezra and Nehemiah have presented two eponymous protagonists. But these men are not lone figures. Each in his own way speaks from within Israel's tradition to the Judahites who are structurally

---

[11] See Hag 2:20-23; Zech 3:8; 4:14; 6:9-15.

[12] Tamara C. Eskenazi, *In an Age of Prose. A Literary Approach to Ezra–Nehemiah* (Atlanta, Ga.: Scholars, 1988) 92.

emphasized here as collaborators and interlocutors, citizens who have rights before the nobles, their debt-holders. Chapter 7 ends with the Judahites settled and accounted for in their towns, ready for the next event. Their opponents are self-destructive, talking at cross-purposes to their own plans.

The language of the two leaders demonstrates their importance but also qualifies it. They speak like the prophets and Moses, and they address the Law. But they are not themselves messiahs, prophets, or heroes in the classic biblical style. Prophecy now abides in them, the leaders, not in those wild figures like Jeremiah who dared to rebuke the kings before the Exile. Now the traditions are continued in a structured, socialized form that, for Ezra–Nehemiah, does not diminish their power. Rather it adapts it for new social and political realities.

Perhaps the most telling sentence in these chapters is that the people prayed and also set a guard (4:9). To believers such as these whose faith is pragmatic, sincere, and grounded, the Law will now be proclaimed.

9:1   Now on the twenty-fourth day of this month, the sons of Israel
were assembled
with fasting
and in sackcloths,
and with earth upon them (i.e., their heads).

9:2   And the Israelites (lit. "seed of Israel") separated themselves
from all foreigners,
and stood
and confessed their sins
and the iniquities of their fathers.

9:3   And they stood up in their place
and read from the book of the law of YHWH their God for a
fourth of the day;
for [another] fourth they made confession (lit. "confessed")
and worshiped YHWH their God.

9:4   Upon the stairs of the Levites stood Jeshua,
and Bani,
Kadmi-el,
Shebaniah,
Bunni,
Sherebiah,
Bani,
and Chenani;
and they cried with a loud voice to YHWH their God.

9:5   Then the Levites,
Jeshua,
Kadmi-el,
Bani,
Hashabneiah,
Sherebiah,
Hodiah,
Shebaniah,
and Pethahiah said,
"Stand up
and bless YHWH your God from everlasting to everlasting.
Blessed be (lit. "they will bless") your glorious name (lit. "the
name of your glory")
[which is] exalted above all blessing and praise.

9:6   You are he, YHWH, you alone;
you have made the heavens,

the heaven of heavens,
and all their host,
the earth
and all that is on it,
the seas
and all that is in them;
and you give life to (lit. "make live") all [of them];
and the host of the heavens to you bows down.

9:7   You are he, YHWH, the God
who chose Abram
and brought him forth out of Ur of the Chaldeans
and placed [upon him] the name Abraham;

9:8   and you found his heart faithful before you,
and made with him the covenant to give the land of the
Canaanite,
the Hittite,
the Amorite,
the Perizzite,
the Jebusite,
and the Girgashite
—to give [it] to his seed;
and you have fulfilled your promise (lit. "raised your word"),
for you are righteous.

9:9   And you saw the affliction of our fathers in Egypt
and heard their cry at the Red Sea,

9:10   and performed signs and wonders against Pharaoh
and all his slaves
and all the people of his land,
for you knew
that they acted presumptuously against our fathers (lit.
        "them");
and you got yourself a name, as [it is known to] this day.

9:11   And the sea you divided before them,
so that they went through the midst of the sea on dry land;
and you cast their pursuers into the depths,
as a stone into mighty waters.

9:12   By a pillar of cloud you led them in the day,
and by a pillar of fire in the night
to light for them the way
in which they should go.

9:13   Upon Mount Sinai you came down
and spoke with them from the heavens
and give them right ordinances

	and laws of truth, good statutes and commandments,
9:14	and your holy sabbath you made known to them, and commandments and statutes and a law you commanded them by the hand of Moses your slave.
9:15	Bread from the heavens you gave them for their hunger and water from [the] rock you brought forth for them, for their thirst, and you told them to go in to possess the land which you had sworn (lit. "raised your hand") to give them.
9:16	But they (and?) our fathers acted presumptuously and stiffened their neck and did not obey (lit. "listen to") your commandments;
9:17	they refused to obey, and did not remember the wonders which you performed among (lit. "with") them; but they stiffened their neck and determined (or appointed a leader? lit. "gave a head") to return to their slavery in Egypt (?, lit. "in their rebellion"). But you are a God ready to forgive (lit. "[of] forgivenesses"), gracious and merciful, slow to anger and abounding in lovingkindness, and did not forsake them,
9:18	even when they had made for themselves a molten calf and said, 'This is your God who brought you up out of Egypt,' and had committed great blasphemies,
9:19	you in your great mercies did not forsake them in the wilderness; the pillar of cloud did not depart from them by day [which] led them in the way, nor the pillar of fire by night [which] lighted for them the way by which they should go.
9:20	Your good spirit (or: wind) you gave to instruct them, and your manna you did not withhold from their mouth, and water you gave them for their thirst.

9:21   Forty years you sustained them in the wilderness,
        and they lacked [nothing];
        their clothes did not wear out
        and their feet did not swell.

9:22   And you gave them kingdoms and peoples,
        and allotted to them [every] corner (?);
        so they took possession of the land of Sihon
        —the land of the king of Heshbon
        and the land of Og king of Bashan.

9:23   Their descendants you multiplied as the stars of the heavens,
        and you brought them into the land
        which you told their fathers to enter and possess.

9:24   [So] the descendants (lit. "sons") went in
        and possessed the land,
        and you subdued before them the inhabitants of the land,
        the Canaanites,
        and gave them into their hands,
        [with] their kings
        and the peoples of the land,
        that they might do with them
        as they would (lit. "according to their favor").

9:25   And they captured fortified cities
        and a rich (lit. "fat") land,
        and took possession of houses full of all good things (goods?),
        cisterns hewn out,
        vineyards,
        olive orchards
        and fruit trees (lit. "of food") in abundance;
        so they ate,
        and were satisfied,
        and became fat,
        and delighted themselves in your great goodness.

9:26   Nevertheless they were disobedient
        and rebelled against you
        and cast your law behind their back
        and your prophets they killed,
        who had warned (or: testified to) them in order to turn them
            back to you,
        and they committed great blasphemies.

9:27   Therefore you gave them into the hand of their oppressors,
        and they oppressed them;
        and in the time of their oppression
        they cried to you

and you from the heavens heard them;
and according to your many mercies
you gave them saviors
and they saved them from the hand of their oppressors.

9:28   But after (lit. "as") they [had] rest
they did evil again (lit. "returned to do evil") before you,
and you abandoned them to the hand of their enemies,
so that they had dominion over them;
yet when they turned
and cried to you,
from the heavens you heard,
and you delivered them according to your mercies many times.

9:29   And you warned (or: testified to) them in order to turn them
back to your law.
Yet those ones—they acted presumptuously
and did not obey your commandments,
but against your ordinances, they sinned against them—
which a person does
and thus lives by them,
and turned a stubborn shoulder
and their neck they stiffened
and would not obey (lit. "listen").

9:30   You bore with them (lit. "pulled on them") many years,
and warned them (or: testified to them) by your spirit,
by the hand of your prophets;
yet they would not give ear.
Therefore you gave them into the hand of the peoples of
    the lands.

9:31   Nevertheless in your great mercies you did not make an
    end of them
or forsake them;
for a gracious and merciful God are you.

9:32   Now therefore, our God,
the great, mighty, and fearsome God,
[who] keep the covenant and (lit. "the") lovingkindness,
let not all the hardship [seem] little to (lit. "before") you
that has come upon us (lit. "found us"),
upon our kings,
our princes,
our priests,
our prophets,
our fathers,
and all your people,

since the time of the kings of Assyria until this day.

9:33 Yet you have been just (or: in the right) in all that has come
upon us,
for you have dealt faithfully (lit. "[in] truth you have done")
and we—we have acted wickedly;

9:34 our kings,
our princes,
our priests,
and our fathers have not kept (lit. "done") your law
or heeded your commandments
and your warnings (or: testimonies)
which you gave (lit. "warned or testified to") them.

9:35 They—in their kingdom, and in your great goodness
which you gave them,
and in the broad and rich land
which you set before them—
they did not serve you;
and they did not turn from their wicked works.

9:36 Behold,
we are this day slaves;
[in] the land
that you gave to our fathers in order that we eat its fruit
and its good gifts,
behold, we are slaves on it.

9:37 And its manifold yield [goes] (lit. "is made manifold")
to the kings
whom you have set over us
because of our sins;
they also over our bodies have power,
and over our cattle at their pleasure,
and in great distress are we."

Chapter Eight
NEHEMIAH 8–10

Introduction

By the sinuous path of its repetitions, reversals, and paralleled patterns the Book of Ezra–Nehemiah now arrives at its peak, the proclamation of the Law. The people's greater receptivity to the Law has prepared for this moment, a context achieved by the restoration of worship at the rebuilt altar and Temple, and the regeneration of society through purifying the families and collaborating in the building of the walls. The Law is now heard by the people for whose reform and forgiveness Ezra had prayed in Ezra 9. He was last seen rising from his prostration before the Temple. His reappearance now helps cleave together these historically separate steps in the Restoration.

The various movements in the book have been signaled with lists of the involved groups (Ezra 2, 8, 10; Nehemiah 3, 7). Now "all the people gathered together (lit. "as one man")" (Neh 8:1).

Proclamations, letters, and messages have prompted and conveyed the action. Communication climaxes here in YHWH's self-expression through the scroll of the Law. Ezra is a "scribe skilled in the law of Moses which YHWH the God of Israel had given" (Ezra 7:6). His sermon-prayer in Ezra 9 was his own free association of legal and prophetic texts. Now he reads the Law, the first "liturgy of the word" on record![1] Ezra 1 began "to fulfill the word of YHWH from the mouth of Jeremiah." The book completes the shift from the sanctity of the oral to that of the written.[2] But its words, fixed there on parchment, are not repeated for us. The Law is not the final point of the book.

---

[1] Bernhard Lang, "From Prophet to Scribe: Charismatic Authority in Early Judaism: An Essay in Biblical History and Sociology," *Monotheism and the Prophetic Minority*. The Social World of Biblical Antiquity Series 1 (Sheffield: Almond, 1983) 146.

[2] Tamara C. Eskenazi, *In an Age of Prose. A Literary Approach to Ezra–Nehemiah* (Atlanta, Ga.: Scholars, 1988) 191.

Rhetorical Situation

Much scholarly opinion would put the original situation of the reading ceremony elsewhere in the book. Coming canonically here in Nehemiah 8 it becomes part of a new hermeneutic for its own interpretation. The important point here is not the stipulations of the Law as read: these details are omitted in this telling of the event. The first question is its reception—how the Law, designed as a constitution for a sovereign realm, can be observed afresh in a subject province of a pagan empire.[3] How can it be proclaimed in a way that is current and engaging but at the same time free from the vicissitudes of Israel's political fortune?

Ezra and Nehemiah stand together on the dais. Traces in the Hebrew text seem to show that the two leaders have been brought together redactionally at this point. An essential part of the theological shaping of Ezra–Nehemiah is that Ezra's reforms in Ezra 7–9 and Nehemiah's work in Nehemiah 1–6 find their full meaning only here in their joint appearance before the scroll of the Law.[4] The two very different figures have spoken and acted in ways that modulated Israel's expectations of leadership in its straitened political reality. The Persian occupation does not allow Israel to enjoy both political independence and Yahwistic faith.

In Ezra 10, then, Ezra disappears lest the people rely on him too much as a political or religious savior, and it is not immediately clear in ch. 8 that Nehemiah is no longer the narrator, although his Memoir has not ended. Before, the two leaders were kept apart but shared the language of the prophets and Moses. Now they stand together but in the text they have no words of their own until after Ezra reads the Law (Neh 8:9). Our attention—and Israel's hope—is projected onto the level of the people.

The people's reception of the Law becomes the paradigm for Israel's faith. Although not politically powerful, Israel can have an autonomous faith that is sincere about conversion and structured within tradition. Ezra and Nehemiah cannot keep the people from sinning again, as we will see in the remaining chapters. But their rhetoric, over against their enemies, has put into motion an interpretive mechanism that holds the Law before the people as the continuous vehicle for conversion. The Law is adaptable, comprehensible, and accessible.

---

[3] H. G. M. Williamson, *Ezra, Nehemiah* (Waco, Tex.: Word Books, 1985) 298.

[4] Brevard S. Childs, *Biblical Theology of the Old and New Testaments. Theological Reflection on the Christian Bible* (Minneapolis: Fortress, 1993) 635.

Speakers

The book rarely describes Ezra and Nehemiah in reference to one another. They are side by side only here. Their titles are given: governor for Nehemiah, scribe and priest for Ezra. The effect of placing them together here is to show that the two faces of Israelite society now meet in Y<small>HWH</small>'s Law. They are twinned religious and civil authorities, as Zerubbabel and Jeshua were before.[5] Both pairs of men stress the same themes: all four have Persian mandates, face local opposition, and insist on separation from the people of the land. Zerubbabel and Jeshua vanished from the history altogether. Ezra and Nehemiah do not disappear yet, but a debt now comes due to the tradition out of which they have spoken. Literally they yield the stage to it in the form of the scroll of the Law.

"They told the scribe Ezra to bring the book" (Neh 8:1). With no clear antecedent the pronoun "they" implies all the people.[6] He, Ezra, reads the Law in 8:3, but in 8:8 "they [the Levites] read from the book, from the law of God, so that the people understood the reading." (Whether this adjunct of meaning is by translation, paraphrase, or audible diction is unclear.) The two leaders and the Levites tell the people not to mourn in 8:9, 10, but the forms of the verb "to tell" are singular.[7] Some Levites named on a second, variant list invite the people to pray.

In the Hebrew text it is unclear who says the long prayer later (9:6-37) or even where it starts.[8] From the Septuagint, the Greek translation, some translations like the NRSV add "And Ezra said" to 9:6. But arguably Ezra would have featured more prominently in the first verses of ch. 9 if he were the maker of such a long prayer.[9] It is reasonable but

---

[5] Judson R. Shaver, "Ezra and Nehemiah: On the Theological Significance of Making them Contemporaries," in *Priests, Prophets and Scribes: Essays on the Formation and Heritage of Second Temple Judaism in Honour of Joseph Blenkinsopp*, eds. Eugene Ulrich et al. JSOT.S 149 (Sheffield: JSOT Press, 1992) 83–85. Nehemiah 12:26 speaks of "the days of the governor Nehemiah and the priest Ezra, the scribe." In 12:36 they walk with groups in opposite directions. See Neh 12:1 and Ezra 2:2 for the only further reference in each book to the other leader, by simple name only.

[6] David J. A. Clines, *Ezra, Nehemiah, Esther* (Grand Rapids: Eerdmans, 1984) 182.

[7] As is the verb "to stand" in 9:4, meant of all the Levites. Plural nouns may govern singular verbs in Hebrew, a grammatical possibility that further frustrates translation.

[8] Are the Levites saying just the first sentence in 9:5, the imperative for the people to stand and bless Y<small>HWH</small>? Do they go on to v. 5b: "Blessed be your glorious name [which is] exalted above all blessing and praise"? Or do they also say 9:6 and rest of the chapter: "You are he, Y<small>HWH</small>, you alone"? Translations vary.

[9] Williamson, *Ezra, Nehemiah* 304.

uncertain that the Levites are the speakers since they already have the floor.

The prayer is unattributed, and so its persuasive power cannot be based on the authority of the speaker, unlike Ezra's prayer in Ezra 9. If the speakers are the Levites they represent the opinion of all the people since immediately afterward, speaking in the first person plural, the people make a firm agreement. Unusually for such documents, we learn of the signatories before the stipulations of the pact. The leaders sign it, but also "the rest of the people" (10:28).

The effect of these syntactical and grammatical vagaries is to preserve the traditional hierarchies but flatten any accent on personalities or command structures. Placed together, Ezra and Nehemiah are seen to share success in their reforms, but their rhetorical presence is muffled. When he first arrived in Jerusalem Ezra did not speak. Now his first words are the Law, and they are not recorded. The Persian king empowered Ezra to make YHWH's Law the writ of the land. Now all the people willingly gather around the Law and submit themselves to it, repenting of their neglect.

In Ezra 4 we asked how one can understand the world and the divine will if, as here, YHWH does not intervene overtly in human affairs. Ezra was introduced as a leader whose will was united to YHWH's. He showed the ideal congruity between action and faith, and his leadership and Nehemiah's replaced that of Sheshbazzar and Jeshua. Now he and Nehemiah let the Law speak first and the people act first. This prayer is a rhetorical demonstration that the people can live faithfully in the imperfect world. This, then, is how faith fits into a religiously reformed but politically subject society whose history has been on one level a story of military defeat but, on another, the medium of YHWH's revelation.

What this "Law" was and whether Ezra adapted it we cannot know. Scholars debate how it might relate to the law that Ezra studied and imposed in the king's name in Ezra 7:10, 25. It and the "book of Moses" in Ezra 6:18 are the two documents of the many in this book that speakers cannot strategically reword or subvert because no part of them is quoted.

The people are now single-minded and enterprising. It is they who ask Ezra to bring the Law to their plenary assembly that unusually includes women and children too. The next day the leaders seek him out to study the Law (8:13). There they discover the prescriptions for the Festival of Booths and they, not Ezra, issue an edict for its general observation. Then on the twenty-fourth day of the month, the people assemble for a liturgy of fasting, reading, and confession without the mention of Ezra or Nehemiah (9:1-5). Their activity as a community institutes the readings of the scroll and then brings on a communal response to it in writing (Nehemiah 10).

Not surprisingly, the book's most frequent use of the Hebrew word for "people" is here in Nehemiah 8 where in its eighteen verses it occurs fifteen times, all but twice in the first dozen verses.[10] The expression "all the people" recurs eleven times in the chapter. Such a density of repetition has no parallel in the book. Each time the people are the actor or the subject.

In Nehemiah 6–7 the wall was the object of activity but not the center of the rhetoric. There the situating of the leaders within the light and shade of tradition was the point. Now it is the free hold of the people over that tradition in the form of the Law, the renewed inheritance that they have appropriated as their guide in the time of foreign occupation. In Ezra 7 the people could know YHWH's will simply because Ezra's will was united to it. We have seen how his and Nehemiah's rhetoric dialogued with tradition. Now the leaders' voices give way to it as embodied in the Law. Similarly, their initiative in the action yields to the people's.

In Ezra–Nehemiah no emissary of God speaks in the name of YHWH as Moses once did. The loss of that grace is made up for by two virtual equivalences. That is, YHWH himself is the content of the Law, and a return to it is a return to him. The strength and alternation of emotions suggest that the Law and its construal are also paralleled. The people cried as they listened to the Law and rejoiced to have understood it (8:9, 12). Although the first reaction of the people was to weep for their sins, a joyful celebration precedes the prayer of penance because the Law is a good gift. But divine authority must be explained and understood for it to give life.[11]

Rhetorical Audience

The prayer is of course addressed to YHWH, but the uncertainty over its speaker means that the broader audience that overheard it is also hard to identify. This prayer is unlike Ezra's, to which we know the people listened and whose rhetoric was pitched to them (Ezra 9). Here the Levites make the prayer for the people, or the people do so themselves. That this climax of the book should be a prayer with no evident audience but YHWH aims the focal point around him in ways that the rhetorical strategies will sharpen. It also opens the prayer to

[10] Neh 8:1, 3, 5 (3x), 6, 7 (2x), 9 (3x), 11, 12, 13, 16.
[11] Williamson, *Ezra, Nehemiah* 293.

us, the current audience, especially since it describes cycles of sin and mercy continuing through all history.

Rhetorical Strategies

It is true to precedent that the people's fuller response to Ezra's reading of the Law should be an act of worship and a prayerful review of their history. Ezra entered the book with a mandate to restore the instruments of worship. Reading the scroll, his last activity, now allows the people to learn and enact the festival prescriptions. He began by proclaiming a fast and doing penance (Ezra 8:21; 9:3-5). He ends by urging rest and celebration.

Until this point every project in the Restoration has met with opposition from foreigners. In Ezra 4–5 the malicious rhetoric of the enemies' letters to the king decried the Judahites' history. Here another account of their past is just as condemning, but it is their own. The difference between the speakers impels us to credit this second version and honor the people's candor.

The Levites explained the Law that explains their past—according to the prayer the Law becomes the hermeneutic of salvation history. In rhetorical terms the Law becomes a *topos* or "topic" in the prayer, an element of proof, especially a general premise allowing one to establish an argument. Such "topics" represent the ways the mind works to generalize, classify, analyze, and synthesize what it perceives. History is described as the actualization of the Law,[12] and the Law is in turn the reflection of YHWH. To put it another way, the Law reveals YHWH and interprets history. The prayer completes the point made in Ezra 5–6 that the divine will is the only true measure of reality.

The species of the rhetoric is a mixture of epideictic, the chief characteristic of which is praise or blame, and deliberative, in which the author wants to persuade the audience to take some action in the future.[13] That is, the prayer's first purpose is to praise YHWH. Second, it persuades the people to ratify the agreement. The deliberative rhetoric accents their freedom of choice. The main method of deliberative speech is inductive example, here the history of YHWH's mercy to the

---

[12] Tamara C. Eskenazi, "Ezra–Nehemiah: From Text to Actuality," in *Signs and Wonders: Biblical Texts in Literary Focus*. Ed. J. Cheryl Exum. SBL.SS 18. (N.p.: Scholars, 1989) 166.

[13] The other species or kind of rhetoric is judicial when the author is seeking to persuade the audience to make a judgement about events occurring in the past. Nehemiah's speeches in Nehemiah 4–7 were also deliberative.

Israelites. The chief strategy of epideictic is amplification, hence the details of this history.

We saw that Ezra's words were in the mode called "ethos," relying on his convincing qualifications as a wise scribe and a man of God (Ezra 7; 9). Nehemiah used "pathos" to move the king to send him to Jerusalem and the people to build the wall (Nehemiah 2; 4). The Levites here are without authority or character. In fact, as we saw, the attribution of the prayer to them or anyone is unclear. Fittingly therefore they use logos, argumentation by reasoning or "near-reasoning" that does not rely on their character or standing. By the people's recommitment to it in ch. 10 the Law is renewed, like the people themselves. What light does it shed on history? The prayer of penance mentions no heroic kings and promises no perfect future. It does not even recall the Return from Exile. Instead it addresses the contradiction that the chosen people are punished. (The rhetorical term is "incompatibility.")

Solidarity with the ancestors in faith means that YHWH's promises to them are valid now, but this generation also then shares in the guilt of the past.[14] The point is "quasi-logical," a "double hierarchy." That is, a scale of values between certain terms is attached to another scale of values already admitted. We accept the history of Israel's covenant with YHWH; therefore we accept the reasons for the current plight of the people. Schematically:

- argument: the ancestors > YHWH;
- thus: this generation > YHWH.

This argument starts proleptically with the immediate association of this generation's sins and those of their ancestors in 9:2: they "stood and confessed their sins and the iniquities of their fathers."

At the same time YHWH is called "their God" repeatedly (9:3 [2x], 4.) "You are he, YHWH, you alone; you have made the heavens. . . . You are he, YHWH, the God who chose Abram and brought him forth . . . you are a God ready to forgive (lit. "[of] forgivenesses"), gracious and merciful . . ." (9:6-7, 17). Once the historical perspective to which we have been predisposed by earlier discourses establishes the benevolent identity of YHWH we must explain the past and present trials of the Judahites as their own fault. "Yet you have been just (or: in the right) in all that has come upon us, for you have dealt faithfully (lit. "[in] truth you have done") and we—we have acted wickedly." In terms of another dissociation or *distinguo* they who should be "slaves" of YHWH like Moses preferred to be "slaves" of the Egyptians and are

[14] J. G. McConville, *Ezra, Nehemiah, and Esther* (Philadelphia: Westminster, 1985) 125.

now "slaves" of the Persians (9:14, 35, 36 [2x]). In short, YHWH is faithful; the people are not.

The covenant does not guarantee faith: we accept a dissociation between these realities. We are asked to accept as well the full association between the covenant and the people's wellbeing, such that disloyalty to the first harms the second, now and for generations.

The prayer uses "quasi-logical" syllogisms called enthymemes to explain this paradox that YHWH is powerful but his chosen people are enslaved. Enthymemes are "quasi-logical" because the first member (in parentheses) is the proposition that is presumed, not proved:

- (God is just to sinners);
- They are sinners;
- God is just to them.

And

- (All who abandon the covenant deserve punishment);
- They have abandoned the covenant;
- They deserve punishment.

Thus only those who deny that they have sinned can deny that God is good. If they have not sinned, why are they slaves of Persia?

It is an argument of essence. In such a presentation of things anything added to the essence destroys the integrity. The essence of Israel's identity is its relation to YHWH, which sin pollutes. In Ezra 4 the language used by the king and the Judahites' enemies subverted their intentions and demonstrated that Israel's true identity did not derive from human power or relations. Now a definition of the reconstituted Israel becomes clearer.

The sequence is important in understanding the next conclusion. Just before the scroll reading the text says again that they separated themselves from the foreigners as Ezra had asked in his own prayer (Ezra 9; Neh 9:1). The Law is read to those who make confession and who are already gathered in Jerusalem, worshiping and reformed. Unfaithfulness has brought disaster. But the inverse is not necessarily true in Ezra–Nehemiah. Nowhere does Nehemiah 9 claim that obedience ensures prosperity and peace. The question is greater than how to live securely.

Who is Israel? And why does Israel not control the Land? Israel can no longer be all those who live in the Land, because of the hostile foreigners. Nor, because of the Persian Empire, can it be those who rule the Land. Israel is all those who obey the Law and keep from foreigners, some of whose names are listed.[15] It is Abraham's seed (9:8). The

[15] Neh 9:2, 8; 10:28. The list of the nations is an instance of *divisio*, categorizing into kinds or classes, and "apposition," the naming of a thing or person.

situation is the opposite of Gen 17:6 where YHWH would make nations out of his seed. Instead, his seed is now governed by the nations.

The importance of the Land is stressed by the repetition of the Hebrew word, used thirteen times in Nehemiah 9.[16] At the base of God's covenant, which included the promise of land, is Abraham's faithfulness: "I will establish my covenant between me and you and your offspring [lit. "seed"] after you throughout their generations for an everlasting covenant, to be God to you and to your offspring after you." (Gen 17:7). The divine promise rests not just on Abraham's faithfulness but also on that of his descendants. If they return to the Law will they repossess the Land? Political prudence forbids voicing this logical corollary. The prayer refuses to extrapolate from the examples of YHWH's mercy. The Law's power to relieve the Judahites is pragmatically limited. The Law is exalted but also qualified, just as the leadership of Ezra never made the people puppets and he and Nehemiah give over to them now by their initial silence. Instead, the prayer opens the opposite question: if obedience does not always bring blessing, why not?

The answer lies in the book's theology of history. Again the wide province of the book is the relation of power and faith. Rhetorical associations are reinforced between the scroll and the Law, YHWH and the Law, the past and the present, the covenant (9:8, 32), and history. The Law is the divine will, but it is set within time and events. Nehemiah 8–10 refuses a mechanical view of salvation. The Law is not formally positive. History is cyclical, as we will see under "Structure," but it cannot be programmed. The only response to it is trust in YHWH and distrust of oneself in the sense that conversion must be continual. And so, beyond even the Law, beyond even his blessings, YHWH alone is ultimate—the focal point and the source of action, however quiescent he may seem. Israel's life and purpose is YHWH, known through the Law within history but freely sovereign in himself.

Structure

According to Tamara Eskenazi, Neh 8:1–13:31 develops in three phases, each comprising an assembly, a reading, and the implementation of the text.[17]

---

[16] Neh 9:6, 7, 15, 22 (3x), 23, 24 (3x), 30 (plural), 35, 36 of which eight times it is the Promised Land. Gilbert, "La place de la loi" 310 says no other text speaks of land so frequently.

[17] Eskenazi, *Age of Prose* 96.

1. First reading and implementation of the Torah (Neh 8:1-12,
   third-person narration)
   a. assembly in 8:1-3
   b. reading in 8:4-8
   c. implementation: celebration, not lamentation in 8:9-12.
2. Second reading and implementation in 8:13-18
   a. assembly around Ezra and Torah in 8:13
   b. reading in 8:14-15
   c. implementation: celebration of Sukkoth in 8:16-18.
3. Third reading and implementation of Torah in 9:1-37
   a. assembly in 9:1-2
   b. reading in 9:3
   c. implementation: the great prayer in 9:4-37.
4. The result: a written pledge to the Torah and the house of God
   by the community in 10:1-40 (MT 9:38–10:39).

This cyclical structure is mirrored in the description of history in
the long prayer in ch. 9, part of the third implementation of the Torah.
It is a mixture of genres, and all commentators agree that it draws
"without distinction on all the major Pentateuchal sources normally
defined."[18] By implication the people have learned the texts of the Law
well and make free use of them.

Verse 5 is corrupt, and it is impossible to be sure where the injunc-
tion to the people ends and the prayer proper begins: "Stand up and
bless YHWH your God from everlasting to everlasting. Blessed be your
glorious name . . ." (9:5). Without more introduction than this, the
prayer turns to the *narratio,* the second section of many speeches, the
one that gives the relevant information (vv. 6-25).[19] It is a series of
praises offered to YHWH. It retraces the events of the Pentateuch up to
the entry into the Land in phrases steeped in biblical traditions but
uniquely combined, especially as a national confession.[20] Then follows
the *confirmatio* or supporting argumentation (9:26-31). Its scheme is
similar to passages in the Book of Judges: a laying out of the cycle of
the rebellion of Israel, the punishment of being handed over to a foreign power, the cry for help, and YHWH's response in mercy and de-

[18] H. G. M. Williamson, *Ezra and Nehemiah* (Sheffield: JSOT Press, 1987) 91.

[19] George A. Kennedy, *New Testament Interpretation through Rhetorical Criticism*
(Chapel Hill and London: University of North Carolina Press, 1984) 48.

[20] H. G. M. Williamson, "Structure and Historiography in Nehemiah 9," in *Panel
Sessions, Proceedings of the Ninth World Congress of Jewish Studies: Biblical Studies and
the Ancient Near East,* ed. Moshe Goshen-Gottstein (Jerusalem: Magnes Press, 1988)
120.

liverance.[21] This pattern is played out three times, or more exactly, two and a half (vv. 26-27; 28; 29-31). The third cycle is broken off: disobedience and punishment are not followed by pleas and deliverance. These elements of the dialectic are instead subsumed into the conclusion where the worshipers describe their own sorry state. The cry to YHWH is their own. They catch themselves up in "the historical continuum by actualizing the cry for help" in confessions, petitions, and laments that speak of their current woes.[22]

This conclusion or *peroratio* begins significantly with the only explicit request in the prayer, "Now therefore . . . let not all the hardship [seem] little to (lit. "before") you" (v. 32). Rhetorical conclusions often fall into various parts: here a recapitulation (v. 32) that sharpens and sums up the main points of the case and a finale (vv. 33-37) that pitches an emotional appeal through the use of words like "behold," "slaves" (2x), "wicked works," "power," the Persians' "pleasure," and "great distress." However charged, its description of the fertile but occupied Land and the people in bondage is not desperate because it is laid into the rhetorical frame of what the past has already revealed of YHWH's character and comes with the concomitant hope that he will once again hear and deliver.

As we saw already at the end of "Rhetorical Strategies," the prayer is not about the Law at all. The first disobedience cited against the Israelites is their refusal to enter the Land in v. 15. (The grumbling in the desert and the Golden Calf are not mentioned until v. 18.) The Law is not mentioned in the introduction, but only at the account of Mount Sinai in vv. 13-14 where no distinction is made between the Decalogue from YHWH and further commandments "by the hand of Moses your slave." The Law is not a code or a set of moral precepts, but an attachment to YHWH.[23] The prophets' fate makes clear that a return to the Law is a return to YHWH: "[they] cast your law behind their back and your prophets they killed, who had warned (or: testified to) them in order to turn them back to you" (v. 26).

The three principal themes are instead the gifts of YHWH, the Land, and the ancestors.[24] They are connected: the Land stands here for all

---

[21] Compare Judg 2:11-16; 3:7-15; 10:6-16. On the cycles see Williamson, "Structure and Historiography," 124.

[22] Williamson, "Structure and Historiography," 125.

[23] Maurice Gilbert, "La place de la loi dans la prière de Néhémie 9," in *De la Tôrah au Messie. Mélanges Henri Cazelles*, eds. Maurice Carrez, Joseph Doré, and Pierre Grelot (Paris: Desclée, 1981) 313.

[24] Gilbert, "La place de la loi," 310: the Hebrew word for "to give" is used fourteen times, the "land" (also translated the "earth") thirteen times, of which eight

YHWH's gifts through the generations. The confessed faults are those of the ancestors who are a "synecdoche" for all Israelites in all times. Synecdoche is an association of two realities through a point of logical necessity. (No generation can exist without its forebears.) The Land is a "metonymy," a rhetorical device that designates one thing by another that is habitually associated with it.[25] The Land plays this representative role here because, as it were, it is the gift that the people have but do not possess. YHWH has given them the Land and they have returned to it, but they are not masters in it. YHWH is not constrained by his gifts.

Judgment is not yet complete in this "theologically exilic situation" marked by "almost unbearable contradiction between God's promise of freedom in the Land and the present subservience to foreigners." "In spite of this, we are making a firm agreement in writing" (Neh 9:38 [MT 10:1]). Here is "a holding-in-tension of present faithful acceptance and future aspiration."[26] Israel's history is a story of YHWH's gift, continually offered but never biddable, as the broken third cycle of the structure makes plain. The rest of the book concerns continuing problems from which Israel is not exempt just because it is recommitted to the Law. Rather the problems of mixed marriages, tithing, and Sabbath profanation occur regardless.

Rhetorical Devices

Diction, the choice of words, is a major rhetorical device here. The verb "to gather" begins each of the major stages of the events in 8:1; 8:13; 9:1. The moments in the prayer are tied together by images of the body that also underline its corporate nature: give ear (v. 30); pulled on (v. 30); shoulder (v. 29); neck (v. 29); hand of enemies (v. 28), of prophets (v. 30), of peoples (v. 30), of Moses (v. 14), of oppressors (v. 27, twice); heart (v. 8); seed (v. 8); give a head (v. 17); raise your hand (v.

---

are for the Promised Land. As for the fathers, "we" meaning the current generation is found only four times, and in the second half.

[25] Olivier Reboul, *Introduction à la rhétorique: théorie et pratique* (2nd ed., Collection 1er cycle Paris: Presses universitaires de France, 1994) 128.

[26] H. G. M. Williamson, "Post-Exilic Historiography," in *The Future of Biblical Studies: The Hebrew Bible*, eds. Richard Elliott Friedman and H. G. M. Williamson. SBL.SS 16 (Atlanta, Ga.: Scholars, 1987) 201, and Williamson, *Ezra, Nehemiah* lii. The translation "in spite of all this" is with Williamson, Blenkinsopp, and Wilhem Rudolph, contrary to Eskenazi and the NRSV "because of all this," Jerusalem Bible "as a result of all this." See Isa 5:25; 9:11; Ps 78:32.

15); feet did not swell (v. 21); behind one's back (v. 26); become fat (v. 25); fat Land (v. 25).[27] Similar phrases recur in each cycle of Israel's history: "gave them into the hand of their oppressors" in the first (v. 27); "abandoned them to the hand of their enemies" in the second (v. 28) and "gave them into the hand of the peoples of the lands" in the third (v. 30). Also note "from the heavens you heard" in the first and second cycles (vv. 26-27).[28] The beginning of the *confirmatio* and the very end of the prayer are also joined by the repetition of what the author probably took to be the same Hebrew root, "distress" in the last line and "oppress" four times in v. 27.[29]

The Israelites are not so different from their enemies the Egyptians, for the Egyptians "acted presumptuously" to Moses as the Israelites did to YHWH (9:10, 16, 29). In similar wordplay, after praying to be like Abraham whose heart was "faithful" the people sign a "firm agreement," a word from the same Hebrew root (9:8, 38 [MT 10:1]).

Chapter 10

The next event, the signing of the agreement, is the response to the three readings and the implementations of the Torah (see "Structure" above).

In an unusual move that emphasizes the role of the people, the signatories are listed first, before the material signed.[30] The groups of signatories in 10:29-30 (MT 10:28-29) broadens the participation to the utmost—Levites, priests, and laity sign. (The names include those priests and Levites familiar from earlier lists. Fourteen of the family names occur in Ezra 2, Nehemiah 7, and Ezra 8, specifying repatriates. Some are wall-builders in Nehemiah 3. Most, however, are new.)

After Ezra's prayer the people agreed only to separate from foreign wives (Ezra 10:3). Now in this climactic moment, with more participation, they undertake a variety of obligations. The individual clauses of the agreement address the major issues of the day. Nehemiah has dealt

---

[27] Such vivid description is *demonstratio*. A similar kind of language is hyperbole: they lacked nothing—even their shoes did not wear out (9:21).

[28] *Conduplicatio* is the repetition of a word or words in succeeding clauses.

[29] Williamson, "Structure and Historiography," 124. The technical term is *polyptoton*, the repetition of words derived from the same root.

[30] Williamson, *Ezra, Nehemiah* 326. "Apposition" is the placing side by side of two coordinate elements, one of which, like the names here, serves as an explanation or modification of the other, here the collective nouns "Levites" and "priests."

with loans on pledge already. The rest receive attention in the remaining chapters:[31]

- mixed marriages (10:30; 13:23-30)
- Sabbath observance (10:31; 13:15-22)
- abandonment of the taking of loans on pledge (10:31; Nehemiah 5)
- the wood offering (10:34; 13:31)
- first fruits (10:35-36; 13:31)
- Levitical tithes (10:37-38; 13:10-14)
- neglect of the Temple (10:39; 13:11)

We saw how the official leadership is quietened in favor of the people's own action. So too the matters for which Nehemiah asked to be remembered are assumed into this national pact:

- he desisted from eating the bread of the governor due to the economic burdens stemming from debt slavery (5:19; 10:31)
- care for the house of God and its services (13:14; 10:39)
- Sabbath observance (13:22; 10:31)
- the cleansing of everything foreign, the duties of priests and Levites, the wood offering, the first fruits (13:31; 10:30, 37-38, 34, 35-36).

Conclusion

With the reading of the scroll and the signing of the pact Ezra–Nehemiah makes complete its turn to the written word. For all the fixity of the documents there are no false assurances in these chapters. The prayer's review of Israel's history demonstrates that YHWH is self-consistent and history is meaningful. The question is how to interpret this meaning.

In Nehemiah 8–10 this interpretation is opposite to that asserted earlier. The tone of the prayer and the repeated references to the Persians as oppressors contrast with the vision in Ezra 1:1 of the era as a fulfillment. Here the Return to the Land is a new but incomplete Exodus because Israel lacks ownership. In Ezra 9, as in Neh 9:35-36, the people are "slaves" of the Persians because they refused to be "slaves" of YHWH. Nonetheless, for Ezra YHWH has not abandoned them, for he has shown them "lovingkindness in the face of the kings of Persia"

---

[31] Williamson, "Post-Exilic Historiography," 196. For simplicity here only the English verse reference is given.

(Ezra 9:9). Here, on the other hand, "the kings dispose of [their] bodies and cattle as they please" (Neh 9:37). In this prayer there is no respite, no Temple, Restoration, or remnant. Ezra's prayer particularly lamented exogamy; here no specific sin is mentioned. There repentance was called for but the prayer finished on a note of mercy (Ezra 9:13-15). Here repentance has already been made, but the prayer ends darkly: "In great distress are we" (Neh 9:37). Are the Persians instruments of the divine, as in Ezra's prayer? Or are they oppressors? Nor has the tension between the divine presence and the reconstruction of the Temple been fully resolved.

We already saw in Ezra 4 and 5–6 concerning the rebuilding of the Temple that alternate accounts of history can run side by side in ways that affirm YHWH's continuing presence. Similar divergences here about the Persians mean that history is reasserted as a medium of YHWH's self-revelation but it is also set within an interpretive frame. The Law is eternal but now transcribed. History is patterned but not predestined.

The center of Israel's life is not the leaders who fall silent or the prophets who were killed (Neh 9:26) or the Land that is taken. The Law is no guarantee of Israel's faithfulness. History is polyvalent. Israel's reconstruction rests only on YHWH, mysterious but known through the resilient balance of structure and event, that is, Law and history. Ezra–Nehemiah depicts life as the living out of the interpreted text of the Law by the historically-minded, covenanted community.

This interpenetration of history and the Law may explain why Ezra–Nehemiah is the end of historiography in the Hebrew Bible. Aside from the Book of Daniel with its anachronisms there is no specific date or event in the Hebrew Bible beyond the reign of Darius II mentioned in Neh 12:22.[32] Brevard Childs remarks that after this no Hebrew or Aramaic book of Scripture tells history in the same way again:

> The history of Israel comes to a close in the Hebrew Bible with the restoration of worship under Ezra. The full significance of this fact has seldom been explored. . . . Obviously, Israel's history with God did not end with Ezra. Yet from the perspective of Israel's tradition, which the shaping of the canon simply registered, the events after Ezra are no longer given an independent place, but attached to earlier writings and according to different genres. This is to say, the relation between history and tradition has been altered. For example, the history of Israel's struggle with the Seleucids has now been rendered in the form of

---

[32] 424–407 B.C.E. David N. Freedman, "The Symmetry of the Hebrew Bible" *StTh* 46 (1992) 92–94.

vaticinia ex eventu and its witness made in the form of Daniel's prophecy in the sixth century. Similarly, events in the Persian period which are most probably reflected in Zechariah and Joel have been fused with an earlier core of writing and the biblical witness no longer functions as history in the same sense as that prior to Ezra. . . . Israel's witness to God which is tied up to a historical sequence breaks off with Ezra. The witness of the continuing encounter with God in the period which follows is made according to a different understanding and by means of other literary techniques.[33]

---

[33] Childs, *Biblical Theology* 164–65. *Vaticinia ex eventu:* prophecies from events.

CONCLUSION

After the abrupt end of the prayer in ch. 9 the furtherance of events is matter-of-fact. Readers used to "happy endings" or grand finales will find the conclusion of Ezra–Nehemiah odd, even alien. In 12:36 Ezra and Nehemiah parade off in opposite directions as part of the ceremony dedicating the walls, but after the signing of the firm agreement in ch. 10 nothing else seems to change. The pact was a commitment to sanctify daily life, and such is the scope of the problems brought forth.

The text itself signals that the material is rearranged: "Now before this" begins one of the episodes that is placed last in the book (13:4). Suddenly a list is made of the priests and Levites who had come up with Zerubbabel and Jeshua at the time of the Return and the building of the second Temple (12:1-9). Then follows another from the next generation including the period of Ezra and Nehemiah and the name of the former (12:12-26). Both epochs are now closed and a new one has begun for Israel. Two passages marked "on that day" signal this completion of Ezra and Nehemiah's conjoined missions (12:44; 13:1).[1]

"Joy" as a verb and noun is used five times in 12:43, the depiction of the ceremony. But by appending Nehemiah's reforms of persistent issues to this signing of the pact Ezra–Nehemiah keeps the reader from confusing the "Golden Age" (as, for example, the Jerusalem Bible subtitles the section 12:44–13:3) with any idyllic community.[2]

As mentioned in the last chapter, the reordering of the episodes makes the reforms subsequent to the decision of the people, so that— *post hoc ergo propter hoc*—Nehemiah seems to act on their agreement. Jerusalem is repopulated, and a ceremonial dedication of the walls long after the end of their reconstruction celebrates the integration

---

[1] Judson R. Shaver, "Ezra and Nehemiah: On the Theological Significance of Making them Contemporaries," in *Priests, Prophets and Scribes: Essays on the Formation and Heritage of Second Temple Judaism in Honour of Joseph Blenkinsopp* (Sheffield: JSOT Press, 1992) 83.

[2] H. G. M. Williamson, *Ezra, Nehemiah* (Waco, Tex.: Word Books, 1985) 377.

achieved among the Law, the wall, the Temple, the people, their past, and their present (Nehemiah 6; 11:1-3; 12:27-43). One people in one city symbolized by the one Temple is an archetype of apocalyptic revelation in the sense of an "unveiling" and completion.[3] The primordial quality of the image reminds us that the book has been treating a mythic theme: the return from exile, the story of homecoming that runs through world literature from Homer's *Odyssey* to a large body of classical Chinese poetry.[4]

However mythic its idea, Ezra–Nehemiah is theologized historiography. It contains documents, letters, dates, and shipping lists. Typologically it refuses the horizons of a lost—or regained—Arcadia: as we have seen, the reformed era is no fantastic paradise. And the book excludes any theological sense of predestination. In the prayer of Nehemiah 9 the cycles of sin and forgiveness are due to the failure of Israel, not any epochal, innate degeneration. Israel forgets YHWH's grace; YHWH remembers, as Nehemiah keeps pleading.

Specifically the application of the purity laws on exogamy demonstrate that the contamination is not inevitable or permanent.[5] The Judahites are not doomed to perpetual alienation from the divine. In the Bible the systemization of blemish and purification laws means that the threat of impurity can be lifted. However xenophobic the Judahites' expulsion of foreigners may seem to us, racial discrimination or superiority is not the point here, nor is the fate of the outsiders. Purity rules are to proclaim the possibility of atonement with YHWH and to enable people to live together. The people's collective self-judgment and decision according to the Law prevent any randomness or personal vendetta in the accusation of blemish. Their misfortunes cannot be the excuse for spiteful blaming or vindication. Pollution cannot be made a weapon.

We have seen how the book draws on the motif of the Exodus. As well as a journey, that departure from Egypt is a model for revolution throughout the Bible and indeed Western culture.[6] Furthermore, observes Northrop Frye:

---

[3] Northrop Frye, *Anatomy of Criticism: Four Essays*, (Atheneum, N.Y.: Atheneum Press, 1966; original publication 1957) 141.

[4] See for example John Simpson, ed. *The Oxford Book of Exile* (Oxford and New York: Oxford University Press, 1995).

[5] The ideas on purity in this paragraph were attributed to Mary Douglas in a conference at Mishkenot Sha'ananim in Jerusalem November 8, 1996. Their application to Ezra–Nehemiah is my own.

[6] This is one of the principal points of Michael Walzer, *Exodus and Revolution* (New York: Basic Books, 1985).

The passages in Ezra and Nehemiah about Jews who are compelled to put away their foreign wives read very unpleasantly in this century of racism; yet the parallel with racism is not quite relevant. Any revolutionary society may have purges that are not necessarily on a racial basis. Closely associated with the purge is the idea of the saving remnant, a curiously pervasive theme in the Bible from the story of Gideon's army in Judges 7 to the exhortations to the seven churches of Asia Minor in Revelation. The feeling that a pure or homogeneous group, no matter how small, is the only socially effective one, and in times of crisis, is the one to be kept for seed, so to speak, until a new age dawns, is an integral part of the revolutionary consciousness.[7]

The making of distinctions is one part of revolutionary reform in Ezra–Nehemiah. The book describes the creation by circumscription of three realities. Physically the rebuilt wall marks the boundaries of the city that is their home and YHWH's in the Temple. The reading of the Law from a scroll is a process of identifying canonically what is "sacred text." The expulsion of the foreigners is the redrawing of the family circle. In the creation of such distinctions the Bible's end comes round to its beginnings.

In the Hebrew and Aramaic Bible Ezra–Nehemiah is the penultimate book, preceding only 1 and 2 Chronicles, but in the best and oldest copies of the ancient text—the Aleppo Codex around 900 C.E. and the Leningrad Codex shortly after 1000 C.E.—Ezra–Nehemiah is the very last. Nehemiah then has the final word in Scripture: "Remember me, O my God, *for good*" (13:31). "God" and "good" are among the predominant words in Genesis, the first book. Genesis ends with the dying words of Joseph: "Even though you intended to do harm to me, God intended it *for good*, in order to preserve a numerous people, as he is doing today" (Gen 50:20). "For good" is the same Hebrew expression in each. In a further correlation in Neh 13:2 the enemy's curse is also turned to a blessing, as Joseph said of his own life.

Genesis opens a world of distinctions and choices. God created by separating light from dark, water from dry land. Humanity's first sin was the failure to distinguish the tree of the knowledge of good and evil from all the other trees in the garden (Gen 2:17). Abel selected the best for his sacrifice to YHWH, unlike his brother. Noah chose pairs among the clean and unclean species and so preserved life. The Hebrew word for "statute" or "regulation" in the sense of the basic stipulations of the Law comes from the root "to carve, to engrave." Thus the divine Law "carves out a boundary, sets up markers, establishes

[7] Northrop Frye, *The Great Code. The Bible and Literature*, (New York and London: Harcourt Brace Jovanovich, 1981) 119.

special domains, all for the purpose of separating the ordered cosmos" from the void.[8]

The differentiations made in Ezra–Nehemiah are of a more pragmatic order, but they close Scripture within the same moral universe. The paradox of Persia's rule over the reformed chosen people is not resolved but rather thrown out into the broader, sharper perspective of the covenant in which the Eternal is known through the mundane, and faithful life consists in daily selecting God-decreed values over human appetites. Daily problems continue, but "deepened at their true level," as a modern rabbinical author says of the Law's purpose.[9]

It is another argument by "double hierarchy" where one scale of values already admitted leads to the acceptance of another:

- argument: differentiations > creation
- thus: differentiations > reformation

Or, in an even simpler rendition of Israel's experience:

- argument: YHWH's choice > Israel
- thus: Israel's choice > YHWH

Such a line of argumentation presupposes an enthymeme:

- (YHWH makes himself known through history.)
- Israel knows history.
- therefore Israel knows YHWH.

These are rhetorical formulations for what Jacob Neusner calls Scripture's "historiography as a code of mythic reflection."[10] Or as Northrop Frye puts it, "The metaphors of creation and apocalypse, at the beginning and end of the Bible, mean that in the presence of God the past is still here and the future already here."[11] History is told from the center of Israel's existence—its relation to YHWH, whether it is the first history in Genesis or the account of Jerusalem's politics in Ezra 4–5. Analogously, in the book's geography the Temple is the center of Jerusalem to which the people gather and around which the walls are built.

[8] *Hoq* from *haqaq*. Joseph B. Soloveitchik, *Halakhic Man*, trans. Lawrence Kaplan (Philadelphia: Jewish Publication Society, 1983) 103.

[9] Joseph B. Soloveitchik, *The Lonely Man of Faith* (New York: Doubleday, 1992; original publication 1965) 15.

[10] Jacob Neusner, "Beyond Myth, after Apocalyptic: The Mishnaic Conception of History," in *The Social World of Formative Christianity and Judaism: Essays in Tribute to Howard Clark Kee*, eds. Jacob Neusner et al. (Philadelphia: Fortress, 1988) 91.

[11] Northrop Frye, *The Double Vision. Language and Meaning in Religion* (Toronto: University of Toronto Press, 1991) 48.

This is a spiritual vision of meaning beyond flux, of "the world not as manifestation . . . [but] as essence . . . as the palpable handiwork of God and his dominion." (So we quoted Jon Levenson[12] in the chapter on Ezra 5–6.) In such a vision humanity becomes a partner with the Creator in the work of renewal.

Such a view of the world subverts those triumphalists for whom the covenant must be a guarantee of Israel's victory. The Book of Exodus is an archetype of salvation by the revolutionary overthrow of the oppressor. Ezra–Nehemiah borrows from its language and imagery, but it casts them in another model of theology beyond Exodus. Like the "Suffering Servant" passages in Isaiah, it has a theology of endurance for believers who are despised minorities in society, or the poorest migrants and refugees today who have no "promised land" to welcome them.[13] On the one hand, it declares that faith is freed from the state and can flourish without sovereignty over the land. The reward of fulfilling the Law is the grace of the Law itself. On the other hand, faith is not a quest for the unworldly: revelation in tradition is accessible and applicable for the common good.

Foreigners figure large in the book: key themes are YHWH's use of alien rulers, separation from outsiders, and the opposition of the foreign people of the land. Whatever the sad historical facts of their treatment may have been, foreigners are representational here in their rhetorical role. They are the counterpoint to the Judahites—the defining contrast, that which is not chosen in order that YHWH might be central.

These distinctions are balanced by the associations set up rhetorically. There are:

- Faith and community.
- Redemption and worship.
- Worship and memory.
- Identity and a mission. Sacred separation alone is not enough.
- Future and tradition.
- Responsibility and freedom: the question of mixed marriages.
- Purity and commitment.
- Faithfulness to the Law and passion for it.
- The Law and the Temple.
- Ezra and YHWH.

[12] Jon D. Levenson, *Sinai and Zion. An Entry into the Jewish Bible* (Minneapolis: Winston, 1985) 142.

[13] Bruce C. Birch, *Let Justice Roll Down: The Old Testament, Ethics and Christian Life* (Louisville: Westminster/John Knox, 1991) 284; Daniel L. Smith, *The Religion of the Landless: The Social Context of the Babylonian Exile* (Bloomington, Ind.: Meyer-Stone Books, 1989) 197.

- Ezra and Nehemiah.
- Ezra, Nehemiah, and the Persian rulers.
- The transitory and the sacred.
- The first audience of the time and us, the current audience of the book.

These relations and distinctions point to the fundamental question, which itself involves discreet but not separate realities. It is the theological question of how to know God and thus act faithfully in the changed world, and more specifically how faith relates in new ways to power and leadership.

Nehemiah returns to Persia: leadership is not the highest good. The law is proclaimed to the people who have been made ready to receive it. That is, attention is paid to the condition of the recipients of the Law just as this commentary has paid attention to the auditors of the rhetoric.

As mentioned in the Introduction, such rhetorical analysis is useful but not uniquely so. At the conclusion of this exercise it is worthwhile to isolate what resists its methodology and so to use rhetorical criticism to clarify outstanding questions.

- To what extent are the rhetorical effects real but unintended? To what extent did the rhetorical aims of the the author and redactor direct the arrangement of the book?
- Is it possible to sit loose to the question of transcultural influence in rhetoric or universal models of discourse?
- Although rhetorical analysis alone cannot answer historical-critical questions, it does invite us to consider whether a very late date for the redaction would place the book in the Hellenistic period and thus under the influence of Greek rhetorical style.
- Among other historical questions, what was the actual fate of the foreigners and who were the people of the land? How do they relate to the Samaritans?
- Since the current scholarly tendency is to assign a late date to the final redaction of many other parts of the Hebrew Bible, how does the theology of Ezra–Nehemiah, as seen through rhetorical criticism, help illuminate the rest of Scripture?
- How does the reform of the people while still in subjugation relate to the deuteronomic theology of just retribution in which the godly are rewarded? How much of Deuteronomy was known then, and in what form?
- How lively then was the influence of Leviticus and its interest in ritual purity? Was it at play in the shunning of the foreigners?
- How does the book speak to the various eschatological tendencies of the day?

- How does it relate to wisdom traditions? Is the view that the wisdom typology begins with the individualizing of the Law relevant here?[14]
- How does it relate to the prophetic tradition, some of which language the leaders employ? (The minimal interest in the people who remained in the Land at the time of the Exile is a reversal of the prophetic stand that the punishment for sin was deportation, not being left behind.[15])
- More specifically, how does the segregation of the people here relate to the vision of universal salvation in Isaiah? (Indeed in Isa 66:20-21 foreigners are taken as priests and Levites!)
- Does the manner of discourse shed any light on the controverted question of eschatological or apocalyptic elements in Ezra–Nehemiah? Some of the imagery is apocalyptic. But since he does not intervene directly here YHWH is not understandable apart from his people. Does the book promote, deny, or ignore any expectation of a definitive divine intervention? How does it relate to Daniel?
- How does the rhetoric of the book fit into the later apocryphal Greek material, especially Esdras?
- How does the book shed light on a more complete biblical picture of leadership? Unlike in Chronicles there is no mention of David, and Solomon is adduced as a paradigm of sin in Neh 13:26.
- How much did the presentation here of the Law as definitive but socially contextualized influence later Judaism's development of *halakah*, Law as a detailed rule of life?[16]
- Did the political realism of the reforms here influence the political content of the New Testament's idea of the kingdom of God?

Broader Reflections

It is the conclusion of this commentary that Ezra–Nehemiah "makes sense." It has unity and meaning that can cross the distance in time between us and the first audience and bear the indeterminate weight of

[14] Northrop Frye, *The Great Code* 121.

[15] John Rogerson and Philip Davies, *The Old Testament World* (Englewood Cliffs, N.J.: Prentice-Hall, 1989) 161.

[16] *Halakah:* "a legal decision for which there is no direct enactment in the Mosaic law, deduced by analogy and included as a binding precept in the Mishnah" (Oxford English Dictionary).

errors and glosses in the text. We do not have to synthesize the narratives and conflate them historico-critically if we can read them otherwise.

What use we make of the text is a matter for each of us. Perhaps in no other place and time did a rhetorical movement take on a greater role than in ancient Israel in forming the national religion and the nation's perception of itself.[17] It may be worthwhile therefore to set out some points by which rhetorical criticism can link Ezra–Nehemiah to avenues of inquiry of a current and pastoral nature.

- We observed that Ezra–Nehemiah can be a model for the utterly dispossessed for whom a revolution in the Exodus style is a vain hope. It is noteworthy that the New Testament is set in such an experience of impotence, minority membership, and even exile.
- The book is a conservative perspective on faith and the world: family, tradition, and purity are cardinal. But these values are viewed creatively as incentives to reform, without hero-worship or coercion. Does the book inform us about tradition in any way that is valuable in current religion and politics?
- What accommodation, if any, should one make with the past in order to live hopefully with the memory of disaster? Or are Ezra–Nehemiah's "Temple truth" and the strategic rearrangement of documents similar to the "state truth" with which we have sad experience in the twentieth century?
- The Law is proclaimed within an impulse to reform that is powered in part by liturgy. How is this a model for worship, preaching, and community development?
- Can faith communities learn anything from the leadership styles of Ezra and Nehemiah, a priest-scribe and a layman respectively? Ezra, a religious leader, is given temporal power in Ezra 7. Is this a regrettable precedent for religion as a political tool?[18]
- Is it significant for modern faith communities that work on the wall begins before all the sensitive questions of social structure have been resolved? Are we too careful to make everyone "comfortable" before we deal with crises?
- Israel can survive and be reformed without political independence. What light does that shed on the priorities of a nation and community?

[17] Michael V. Fox, "The Rhetoric of Ezekiel's Vision of the Valley of the Bones," in *The Place Is Too Small For Us: The Israelite Prophets in Recent Scholarship* (Winona Lake, Ind.: Eisenbrauns, 1995) 5.

[18] Bernhard Lang, "From Prophet to Scribe: Charismatic Authority in Early Judaism: An Essay in Biblical History and Sociology," in *Monotheism and the Prophetic Minority* (Sheffield: Almond, 1983) 147.

BIBLIOGRAPHY

Alonso-Schökel, Luis. *Cronicas, Esdras, Nehemias*. Los Libros Sagrados 6. Eds. Luis Alonso Schökel and Juan Mateos. Madrid: Ediciones Cristiandad, 1976.

Alter, Robert. "How Convention Helps Us Read: The Case of the Bible's Annunciation Type-Scene," *Prooftexts* 3 (1983) 115–30.

Becker, Joachim. *Esra–Nehemia*. NEB.AT. Eds. Josef G. Plöger and Josef Schreiner. Würzburg: Echter Verlag, 1990.

Betz, Hans Dieter. *Galatians: A Commentary on Paul's Letter to the Churches in Galatia*. Hermeneia. Eds. Frank Moore Cross, Helmut Koester, and others. Philadelphia: Fortress, 1979.

Birch, Bruce C. *Let Justice Roll Down: The Old Testament, Ethics and Christian Life*. Louisville: Westminster/John Knox, 1991.

Bitzer, Lloyd F. "The Rhetorical Situation," *Philosophy & Rhetoric* 1 (1968) 1–14.

Blenkinsopp, Joseph. *Ezra–Nehemiah*. OTL. Eds. Peter Ackroyd et al. Philadelphia: Westminster, 1988.

Bossman, David. "Ezra's Marriage Reform: Israel Defined," *BTB* 9 (1979) 32–38.

Bovati, Pietro, and Roland Meynet. *Le livre d'Amos*. Collection Rhétorique Biblique 2. Paris: Cerf, 1994.

Boynton, Robert S. "Loury's Exodus," *The New Yorker* May 1,1995, 33–41.

Braulik, Georg. *Die Mittel deuteronomischer Rhetorik*. AnBib 68. Rome: Pontifical Biblical Institute, 1978.

Brueggemann, Walter. *The Land. Place as Gift, Promise and Challenge in Biblical Faith*. Overtures to Biblical Theology 1. Eds. Walter Brueggemann and John R. Donahue. Philadelphia: Fortress, 1977.

Caird, G. B. *The Language and Imagery of the Bible*. Philadelphia: Westminster, 1980.

Cangh, Jean-Marie van. "Temps et eschatologie dans l'Ancient Testament." In *Temps et eschatologie: données bibliques et problématiques contemporaines*. Ed. Jean-Louis Leuba. Paris: Cerf, 1994, 17–38.

Childs, Brevard S. *Biblical Theology of the Old and New Testaments. Theological Reflection on the Christian Bible*. Minneapolis: Fortress, 1993.

Cirlot, Juan Eduardo. *A Dictionary of Symbols*. Translated by Jack Sage. London: Routledge & Kegan Paul, 1962.

Clines, David J. A. *Ezra, Nehemiah, Esther*. NCBC. Eds. Ronald E. Clements and Matthew Black. Grand Rapids: Eerdmans, 1984.

_____. "The Nehemiah Memoir: The Perils of Autobiography." In *What Does Eve Do To Help? And Other Readerly Questions to the Old Testament*. Eds. David J. A. Clines and Philip R. Davies. JSOT.S 94. Sheffield: JSOT Press, 1990, 124–64.

Duke, Rodney K. *The Persuasive Appeal of the Chronicler: A Rhetorical Analysis.* JSOT.S 88. Eds. David J. A. Clines and Philip R. Davies. Sheffield: Almond, 1990.

Eskenazi, Tamara Cohn. *In an Age of Prose. A Literary Approach to Ezra–Nehemiah*. Atlanta, Ga.: Scholars, 1988.

_____. "The Structure of Ezra–Nehemiah and the Integrity of the Book," *JBL* 107 (1988) 641–56.

_____. "Ezra-Nehemiah: From Text to Actuality." In *Signs and Wonders: Biblical Texts in Literary Focus*. Ed. J. Cheryl Exum. SBL.SS 18. N.p.: Scholars, 1989, 165–215.

Fensham, F. Charles. *The Books of Ezra and Nehemiah*. NIC. Ed. R. K. Harrison. Grand Rapids: Eerdmans, 1982.

Fishbane, Michael. *Biblical Interpretation in Ancient Israel*. Oxford: Clarendon Press, 1985.

Fox, Michael V. "The Rhetoric of Ezekiel's Vision of the Valley of the Bones." In *The Place Is Too Small For Us: The Israelite Prophets in Recent Scholarship*. Ed. Robert P. Gordon. Sources for Biblical and Theological Study 5. Winona Lake, Ind.: Eisenbrauns, 1995, 176–90.

Freedman, David N. "The Symmetry of the Hebrew Bible." *StTh* 46 (1992) 83–108.

Frye, Northrop. *Anatomy of Criticism: Four Essays*. Atheneum, N.Y.: Atheneum Press, 1966; original publication 1957.

_____. *The Great Code. The Bible and Literature*. New York and London: Harcourt Brace Jovanovich, 1981.

_____. *Words with Power. Being a Second Study of "The Bible and Literature."* San Diego, New York, and London: Harcourt Brace Jovanovich, 1990.

_____. *The Double Vision. Language and Meaning in Religion*. Toronto: University of Toronto Press, 1991.

Galling, Kurt. "Die Proklamation des Kyros in Esra 1." In *Studien zur Geschichte Israels im persischen Zeitalter*. Tübingen: J. C. B. Mohr (Paul Siebeck), 1964, 61–77.

Gilbert, Maurice. "La place de la loi dans la prière de Néhémie 9." In *De la Tôrah au Messie. Mélanges Henri Cazelles*. Eds. Maurice Carrez, Joseph Doré, and Pierre Grelot. Paris: Desclée, 1981, 307–16.

Görg, Manfred. "בזה *bazah*." In *Theological Dictionary of the Old Testament*. Eds. G. Johannes Botterweck and Helmer Ringgren. Revised 2nd ed. Grand Rapids: Eerdmans, 1977, reprint 1988, 2:60–65.

Gunneweg, Antonius H. J. "Zur Interpretation der Bücher Esra–Nehemia: Zugleich ein Beitrag zur Methode der Exegese." In *Congress Volume, Vienna, 1980*. Ed. J. A. Emerton. VT.S 32. Leiden: Brill, 1981, 146–61.

_____. *Esra*. KAT 19/1. Gütersloh: Gerd Mohn, 1985.

_____. *Nehemia*. KAT 19/2. Gütersloh: Gerd Mohn, 1987.

Halpern, Baruch. "A Historiographic Commentary on Ezra 1–6: Achronological Narrative and Dual Chronology in Israelite Historiography." In *The Hebrew Bible and its Interpreters*. Eds. William H. Propp, Baruch Halpern, and David N. Freedman. Biblical and Judaic Studies 1. Winona Lake, Ind.: Eisenbrauns, 1990.

Hurowitz, Victor (Avigdor). *I Have Built You an Exalted House: Temple Building in the Bible in Light of Mesopotamian and Northwest Semitic Writing*. JSOT.S 115. Eds. David J. A. Clines and Philip R. Davies. Sheffield: Sheffield Academic Press, 1992.

Japhet, Sara. "Composition and Chronology in the Book of Ezra–Nehemiah." In *Second Temple Studies: 2. Temple and Community in the Persian Period*. JSOT.S 175. Sheffield: JSOT Press, 1994, 189–216.

_____. "'History' and 'Literature' in the Persian Period: The Restoration of the Temple." In *Ah, Assyria . . . Studies in Assyrian History and Ancient Near Eastern Historiography Presented to Hayim Tadmor*. Eds. Mordechai Cogan and Israel Eph'al. ScrHie 33. Jerusalem: Magnes Press, 1991, 174–88.

_____. "Sheshbazzar and Zerubbabel—Against the Background of the Historical and Religious Tendencies of Ezra–Nehemiah," *ZAW* 94 (1982) 66–98.

Kennedy, George A. *New Testament Interpretation through Rhetorical Criticism*. Chapel Hill and London: University of North Carolina Press, 1984.

Lang, Bernhard. "From Prophet to Scribe: Charismatic Authority in Early Judaism: An Essay in Biblical History and Sociology." In *Monotheism and the Prophetic Minority*. The Social World of Biblical Antiquity Series 1. Sheffield: Almond, 1983, 138–56.

Lanham, Richard A. *A Handlist of Rhetorical Terms. A Guide for Students of English Literature*. Berkeley: University of California Press, 1968.

Lausberg, Heinrich. *Handbuch der literarischen Rhetorik: Eine Grundlegung der Literaturwissenschaft*. 3rd ed. Stuttgart: Franz Steiner, 1990.

Lenchak, Timothy A. *"Choose Life!" A Rhetorical-Critical Investigation of Deuteronomy 28,69–30,20*. AnBib 129. Rome: Pontifical Biblical Institute, 1993.

Levenson, Jon D. "The Temple and the World," *JR* 64 (1984) 275–98.

_____. *Sinai and Zion. An Entry into the Jewish Bible*. New Voices in Biblical Studies 1. Eds. Adela Yarbro Collins and John J. Collins. Minneapolis: Winston, 1985.

Mangan, Celine. *1–2 Chronicles, Ezra, Nehemiah*. OTMes 13. Eds. Carroll Stuhlmueller and Martin McNamara. Wilmington, Del.: Michael Glazier, 1982.

McConville, J. G. *Ezra, Nehemiah, and Esther*. The Daily Study Bible 21. Ed. John C. L. Gibson. Philadelphia: Westminster, 1985.

Molinié, Georges. *Dictionnaire de rhétorique*. Les Usuels de poche 8074. Eds. Mireille Huchon and Michel Simonin. Paris: Librairie générale française, 1992.

Neusner, Jacob. "Beyond Myth, after Apocalyptic: The Mishnaic Conception of History." In *The Social World of Formative Christianity and Judaism: Essays in Tribute to Howard Clark Kee*. Eds. Jacob Neusner et al. Philadelphia: Fortress, 1988, 91–106.

Nodet, Étienne. *Essai sur les origines du Judaïsme: de Josué aux Pharisiens*. Paris: Cerf, 1992.

North, Robert. "Ezra." *ABD*. Eds. David Noel Freedman et al New York: Doubleday, 1992, 2:726–728.

Perelman, Chaïm. "Rhetoric in philosophy: the new rhetoric." In *Encyclopaedia Britannica*. Ed. Philip W. Goetz. 15th ed. Chicago: Encyclopaedia Britannica Co. Ltd., 1991, 26:762–764.

Perelman, Chaïm and Lucie Olbrechts-Tyteca. *Traité de l'argumentation: La nouvelle rhétorique*. 5th ed. Brussels: Editions de l'Université de Bruxelles, 1988; original publication 1958.

Petersen, David L., ed. *The Temple in Persian Period Prophetic Texts*. Second Temple Studies: I. Persian Period. Sheffield: JSOT Press, 1991.

Plöger, Otto. *Theokratie und Eschatologie*. WMANT. Neukirchen: Neukirchener Verlag, 1959.

Porten, Bezalel. "The Address Formulae in Aramaic Letters: A New Collation of Cowley 17." *RB* 90 (1983) 396–415.

Reboul, Olivier. *Introduction à la rhétorique: théorie et pratique*. 2nd ed., Collection 1er cycle Paris: Presses universitaires de France, 1994.

_____. *La rhétorique*. 5th ed. QSJ 2133. Paris: Presses universitaires de France, 1996.

Rogerson, John, and Philip Davies. *The Old Testament World*. Englewood Cliffs, N.J.: Prentice-Hall, 1989.

Shaver, Judson R. "Ezra and Nehemiah: On the Theological Significance of Making them Contemporaries." In *Priests, Prophets and Scribes: Essays on the Formation and Heritage of Second Temple Judaism in Honour of Joseph Blenkinsopp*. Eds. Eugene Ulrich et al. JSOT.S 149. Sheffield: JSOT Press, 1992, 76–86.

Simpson, John, ed. *The Oxford Book of Exile*. Oxford and New York: Oxford University Press, 1995.

Sloane, Thomas. "Rhetoric: Rhetoric in literature." In *Encyclopaedia Britannica*. Ed. Philip W. Goetz. 15th ed. Chicago: Encyclopaedia Britannica Co. Ltd., 1991, 26:758–762.

Smith, Daniel L. *The Religion of the Landless: The Social Context of the Babylonian Exile*. Bloomington, Ind.: Meyer-Stone Books, 1989.

Soloveitchik, Joseph B. *Halakhic Man*. Translated by Lawrence Kaplan. Philadelphia: Jewish Publication Society, 1983.

_____. *The Lonely Man of Faith*. New York: Doubleday, 1992; original publication 1965.

Talmon, Shemaryahu. "Ezra and Nehemiah." In *The Literary Guide to the Bible*. Eds. Robert Alter and Frank Kermode. Cambridge, Mass.: Harvard University Press, 1987, 357–64.

Throntveit, Mark A. *Ezra–Nehemiah*. Interpretation. Ed. Paul Achtemeier. Louisville: John Knox, 1992.

Trible, Phyllis. *Rhetorical Criticism: Context, Method and the Book of Jonah*. Guides to Biblical Scholarship. Ed. Gene M. Tucker. Minneapolis: Fortress, 1994.

Walzer, Michael. *Exodus and Revolution*. New York: Basic Books, 1985.

White, Hayden. *Metahistory: The Historical Imagination in the Nineteenth Century*. Baltimore: Johns Hopkins University Press, 1973.

_____. "Rhetoric and History." In *Theories of History*. Eds. Hayden White and Frank E. Manuel. William Andrews Clark Memorial Library Seminar Papers. Los Angeles: University of California Press, 1978, 3–25.

Williamson, H. G. M. "The Composition of Ezra i–vi." *JThS n.s.* 34 (1983) 1–30.

_____. *Ezra, Nehemiah*. WBC 16. Eds. David A. Hubbard et al. Waco, Tex.: Word Books, 1985.

_____. *Ezra and Nehemiah*. OTGu. Ed. R. N. Whybray. Sheffield: JSOT Press, 1987.

_____. "Post-Exilic Historiography." In *The Future of Biblical Studies: The Hebrew Bible*. Eds. Richard Elliott Friedman and H. G. M. Williamson. SBL.SS 16. Atlanta, Ga.: Scholars, 1987, 189–207.

_____. "Structure and Historiography in Nehemiah 9." In *Panel Sessions, Proceedings of the Ninth World Congress of Jewish Studies: Biblical Studies and the Ancient Near East*. Ed. Moshe Goshen-Gottstein. Jerusalem: Magnes Press, 1988, 117–32.

Witherington, Ben III. *Conflict & Community in Corinth: A Socio-Rhetorical Commentary on 1 and 2 Corinthians*. Grand Rapids: Eerdmans, 1995.

Wuellner, Wilhelm. "Where is Rhetorical Criticism Taking Us?" *CBQ* 49 (1986) 448–63.

SUBJECT INDEX

SCRIPTURE INDEX